The New
Calorie–Neutralizer
Diet

Other Books by Anthony Norvell:

The New Calorie–Neutralizer Diet

ANTHONY NORVELL

Parker Publishing Company, Inc.
West Nyack, New York

Library of Congress Cataloging in Publication Data

Norvell, Anthony.
   The new calorie–neutralizer diet.

   Includes index.
   1. Reducing diets. 2. Low-calorie diet.
3. High-fiber diet. I. Title.
RM222.2.N667 1983   613.2′5   82-22317
ISBN 0-13-611830-5
ISBN 0-13-611822-4 {PBK}

How This Book
Will Help You

I have discovered a new weight-reducing system that can help any overweight person lose 8 to 12 pounds in one week with very little effort. In fact, losing weight with this method is not only easy and safe, but it is actually pleasant. You can even eat up to 4 pounds of certain foods a day and still lose weight!

This new dietary system uses easy-to-get foods, which I call *calorie–neutralizers*, that help blast away fat cells and drive the harmful acid ash out of your bloodstream in record time. You can eat many rich, high-calorie foods such as cream, butter and many types of desserts, which are taboo in most reducing diets, and still lose as many pounds as you desire! Why? Because the foods you eat at each meal—the calorie–neutralizers—actually prevent your digestive tract from metabolizing and absorbing the fat calories by flushing them out of your system before they can be turned into fat deposits. You can eat such a wide variety of foods in this new calorie–neutralizer diet that you will feel as if you are feasting, not fasting!

Most diet systems limit you to a certain number of calories each day; so little, in fact, that you feel constantly hungry. When the hunger-stat is turned on because of the limited amount of food in your intestinal tract, your body screams for food; the carbohydrate, fattening kinds of food that are instantly turned into excess fat. Then you begin to overeat, and with nothing to stop the fat machine from converting those excess calories into fat, you begin to slowly but surely gain weight.

The new calorie–neutralizer diet permits you to eat more than the usual 900 to 1200 calories a day that most diets allow. The foods you will eat are low-calorie, non-fattening calorie–neutralizers. No matter how much you eat of these foods, they

5

cannot put extra fat on your body. The simple reason for this is that most of the calorie–neutralizer foods *take more calories to digest than they give to the body!* In fact, *the more of these foods you eat, the quicker you will lose your excess weight.*

20 AMAZING RESULTS
YOU WILL ACHIEVE WITH
THE NEW CALORIE–NEUTRALIZER DIET

1. You will easily lose from 10 to 50 pounds in the shortest possible time without ever feeling hungry or suffering from weakness or lack of energy. You will lose from 8 to 12 pounds a week on the calorie–neutralizer diet. You can eat such rich foods as bacon and eggs, butter and cream, mayonnaise, steaks and lobster, chicken and fish, as well as tasty salads and two vegetables with each meal, and yet the fat will continue to melt away. The calorie–neutralizer fruits, vegetables and grains permitted on this diet will help neutralize the fat calories you do consume, so they can never add weight to your body. Learn in Chapter 1 how Flora G., who was 48 pounds overweight, used the calorie–neutralizer diet to lose 10 pounds a week, until her weight was back to normal. Flora had no feelings of hunger or weakness, even with that tremendous weight loss!

2. Learn how to use calorie–neutralizer foods that act as catalysts in your diet. They are capable of changing the chemistry of the fat foods you ingest and eliminating them from your body without permitting fat cells to accumulate. Discover the effect of alkaline foods such as high-fiber fruits, vegetables and grains. Learn how the body tends to flush out the fat cells by converting the acid ash into alkaline substances. Linda A. lost weight on the new calorie–neutralizer diet, but she switched to high-calorie fruits and vegetables in her second week, and found she lost only 3 pounds. She lost more weight when she resumed the original calorie–neutralizer list of foods. Chapter 1 tells Linda's story.

3. The calorie–neutralizer diet is especially effective for quick weight loss without causing any stress. "Buffer" foods give a wide variety to your diet so you never tire of the calorie–

neutralizer foods in each day's menu. Chapter 5 lists a variety of breakfasts with such rich foods as bacon and eggs, omelets with Cheddar cheese, mushrooms, diced ham, green peppers and onions—breakfasts that will let you lose weight without making you feel as though you are dieting. A wide variety of other rich foods for lunch and dinner will furnish you with enough calories to maintain your good health. At the same time, the neutralizing effect of the fruits and vegetables will remove the fat calories you might have eaten.

Discover the method Robert D., a truck driver, used to get rid of 50 excess pounds. By having plenty of "buffer" foods, he actually ate more than before, and yet the fat melted away in just four weeks without effort on his part and without ever feeling hungry.

4. You will learn how to receive valuable vitamins for perfect nutrition even while losing weight. Doctors and nutritionists warn that most reducing diets fail to include the minimum daily requirements of essential vitamins in their menus, causing dieters to suffer from vitamin deficiency. You will learn about the calorie–neutralizer foods that include all the essential vitamins in Chapter 6, and find the built-in safety features of the calorie–neutralizer diet that take care of your daily vitamin requirements without expensive food supplements and vitamins. Learn how Diana R. used the calorie–neutralizer foods to supply an important vitamin; lack of the vitamin in her diet had caused her to have two miscarriages. She not only lost 25 pounds of excess weight but, with the help of her new diet, once again became pregnant and had a normal, healthy baby girl.

5. One of the most important differences between the new calorie–neutralizer diet and other diets is that you need never again fear that you will be constantly hungry while losing weight. You will be able to eat up to 4 pounds of delicious and nutritious foods each day. Dan B. gained 80 pounds from eating rich, high-calorie foods; his weight went from 160 to 240 pounds in three years. Chapter 5 tells how Dan was able to shed those 80 pounds without suffering from the hunger pangs which had made him a compulsive eater. His wife Betty went on the same calorie–neutralizer diet and lost 25 pounds.

6. One of the greatest benefits you will derive from the new calorie–neutralizer diet is that you will forever break the vicious carbohydrate habit from which millions suffer. You will learn how to obtain the 60 grams your body needs each day for a balanced diet that will furnish you with carbohydrates, proteins and fats, and yet not make you gain weight. Find out how a romantic actor lost 40 pounds when he broke the carbohydrate habit and went on the new calorie–neutralizer diet. Chapter 7 gives you the extension diet that will permit you to eat many rich, high-calorie foods while you still lose weight. Millie S., 55 pounds overweight, began to eat as many as four calorie-neutralizer vegetables with some low-calorie desserts—she lost that weight in a surprisingly short time without feeling tired or hungry once.

7. Most reducing systems limit the caloric intake from 900 to 1200 calories a day. These are usually low-fat and low-energy foods that do not furnish the body with enough energy to meet the day's expenditure. This leads to fatigue, headaches and other symptoms that usually cause a person to give up the diet and revert to old fattening food habits. In the new calorie–neutralizer diet you will be able to eat up to 1500 and even 2000 calories a day and still lose weight. The reason for this is that the calorie–neutralizer foods take more calories to digest than they give to your body. See in Chapter 5 how Susan L. consumed 3000 calories a day and gained 35 pounds. When she went on the calorie–neutralizer diet, she was able to eat as much as 2000 calories a day of nonfattening foods and easily shed the pounds she had gained.

8. Doctors now know that many diseases are caused by being overweight. Many cases of high blood pressure, heart trouble, diabetes, kidney disorders, arthritis and digestive disturbances are often due to years of dietary neglect and being overweight. Although no claims are made that the new calorie-neutralizer system of dieting will overcome illness, there have been many instances where people have improved physically when they have lost excess weight. Fred S., who was 50 pounds overweight, suffered from many disorders that were attributed to his weight. On the new calorie–neutralizer diet Fred was able to lose the extra pounds and his doctor found that his health was vastly improved. See Chapter 3.

9. Chapter 11 tells how to prepare many new and interesting calorie–neutralizer dishes to help you lose weight. You can even choose the lacto-vegetarian way of life and never again put on weight. However, there are certain vegetables and fruits which have more fat calories that you should not include in a diet to lose weight. Chapter 7 tells how Judy A., who was a vegetarian, still gained 15 pounds over her normal weight while on the calorie–neutralizer diet. She lost the excess pounds without effort, by eliminating the vegetables and fruits that were rich in fat calories, and then went on the extension diet, following her vegetarian way of life.

10. Provision is made on the diet for those who need to lose more than 20 to 30 pounds. You can eat delicious, rich-tasting, but low-calorie foods that will allow you to lose weight while you feast like a gourmet. The delicious recipes given in Chapter 11 can be used to supplement the calorie–neutralizer reducing menus. You can continue to lose anywhere from 30 to 100 pounds, yet never feel restricted in your food intake when you use these delicious recipes. Chapter 11 tells how Cynthia L., a gourmet, gained 65 unsightly pounds before she came into the diet workshop. She was permitted to eat some of the tasty, gourmet-type foods that included shrimp, lobster à la Newburg, crabmeat salads, roasts, stews and omelets. Cynthia never once complained about her diet. She easily and quickly shed the excess pounds and then went on the lifetime extension diet.

11. After just a few days on the calorie–neutralizer diet, you will feel an outpouring of energy and begin to enjoy life more than you ever thought possible before. More important than the physical benefits you will derive will be the psychological changes that occur when you no longer worry about being overweight and unattractive. Discover the vital importance of iron and other essential elements in a diet, which can change your outlook on life and even improve your love life. Teresa A. was only 15 pounds overweight but she felt such fatigue she could hardly get through a day's household chores without collapsing. She had lost all interest in her children and her husband. On the calorie–neutralizer diet, Teresa ate foods rich in iron. She not only lost her excess weight but her outlook on life and marriage radically improved. See Chapter 10.

12. Chapter 12 tells how to go on a lifetime sustaining diet that will never again permit you to gain weight. A wide variety of meats, fishes, poultry, vegetables, grains, fruits, nuts and milk products can be eaten, which are still in the low-calorie range permitted on a normal diet. These calorie–neutralizer foods mixed with the higher fat foods will give you a balanced diet that will fulfill all your daily needs, and keep you from putting on extra pounds. Learn in this chapter how Thelma W.'s weight increased to an incredible 220 pounds in two years, and how she suffered because of it. It was difficult for her to get through each day as she worked for her living. She went on the calorie–neutralizer diet and lost 85 pounds without suffering from fatigue, weakness or hunger-pangs.

13. Discover how calorie–neutralizer foods not only help you reduce quickly and easily, but will improve your love life and marriage. In Chapter 10 you will read how Roland T. was overweight, and had become sexually impotent. On the new calorie–neutralizer diet he not only got rid of his 20 excess pounds, but the minerals and other elements he received gave him back his virility and helped save his floundering marriage. Find out the latest scientific research about such minerals as iron, iodine, calcium, copper and manganese. All play a vital role in your good health. Chapter 10 tells what calorie–neutralizer foods are rich in the minerals your body needs, even when you are of normal weight.

14. Many reducing diets make people highly nervous, irritable and quick-tempered because they are denied the necessary nutrients that feed the nervous system and brain. The calorie–neutralizer diet lets you eat such seemingly rich foods as filet mignon, roast beef, liver, sweetbreads, lamb chops and a wide variety of vegetables and fruits. Yet you will receive more than enough nourishment to feed your body, and you will never succumb to periods of depression and nervousness. Chapter 4 tells how Helen C. overcame her weight problem *and* her terrible nervousness and apprehension at the same time. Although 45 pounds overweight, she immediately began to lose weight on the calorie–neutralizer diet—18 pounds in two weeks. Another two weeks, and she had lost 20 more pounds. In a few more days she was back to her normal 118 pounds without suffering once from the adverse symptoms most dieters experience.

15. In the new calorie–neutralizer diet, you will discover a complete new world of foods that appeal to the taste buds and yet which are so low in calories that you will continue to lose pounds while eating them. You can add pleasure to your dieting with calorie–neutralizer salads, sauces, marinades and even low-calorie mayonnaise. Salad recipes for new combinations of calorie–neutralizer raw vegetables are given in Chapter 9. Learn how to prepare these nourishing, slenderizing salads and begin to benefit immediately from eating them. When Della J. developed alarming symptoms, her doctor told her to reduce. She was able to vary her diet with appetizing salads and lost 30 pounds in a brief period of time.

16. You will be given high-fiber foods, such as grains, vegetables and fruits, that break down the cellulite deposits of the body and remove the acid ash that accumulates from too many high-calorie foods. These high-fiber foods neutralize the rich calories so rapidly that they cannot add fat cells to the body. This increases the rapid action in the digestive tract, removing the fattening calories before they have a chance to build into fatty cells. You will learn in Chapter 3 how Sara M., who was 32 pounds overweight and ate up to 400 grams a day of carbohydrates, was able to lose weight when she went on the calorie–neutralizer diet. She ate cantaloupe, strawberries and watermelon several times a day. In a little more than three weeks these high-fiber, calorie–neutralizers literally melted that fat away.

17. There are other side benefits that come from the calorie–neutralizer diet. You will have higher energy levels because of the balanced nutrition intake. Foods containing all the amino acids and lecithin will be included in the daily menus. These various foods can bring amazing improvements in your love life, increasing sexual enjoyment with your love partner and bringing greater compatibility. Losing weight will help you stimulate sexual activity and increase desire, for the special foods in the calorie–neutralizer diet strengthen and improve the entire body. Scientists have proved that certain foods definitely increase physical efficiency and sexual activity. Learn what these foods are and use them the rest of your life. In Chapter 10 you will see how dietary deficiencies led Wendy H. to gain 55 pounds in weight, with a loss of affection for her husband and her children. A simple correction in her diet not only helped her to lose the weight but she regained her maternal instinct and felt sexual interest once again for her husband.

18. Many Americans suffer from malnutrition, even though they can afford the best food in the world. An unbalanced diet causes many disorders, including tooth decay, receding gums, goiter, skin problems and even serious mental disorders. In reducing with the new calorie–neutralizer diet, and later, on the lifetime sustaining diet, you will be given a balanced food plan that assures you of receiving all the nutritional elements you need to maintain good health and youthful energy the rest of your life. You will be told what foods to include in your daily diet, even when you are not reducing, to bring you nutritional balance without ever again putting on excess weight. Charlotte W. ate many foods that would be considered calorie-rich and lost excess pounds. Chapter 4 tells how she did this and gives two weeks of delicious calorie–neutralizer menus for reducing.

19. You may have tried other reducing systems and found that you were not able to stay on the diet because of the small amount of food you were permitted to eat. This made you feel half-starved all the time and created such anxiety that you simply could not stay on the diet. In the new calorie–neutralizer diet you can eat up to six times a day, if you wish, keeping your stomach full of nonfattening foods. In Chapter 2 learn how Irene S. became 40 pounds overweight on a predominantly carbohydrate diet. In exactly six weeks she lost the weight—without suffering from hunger pangs or any discomfort the whole time she dieted.

20. The sweet-tooth syndrome affects the health of millions of Americans and is responsible for tons of unwanted fat.

Thousands of children are destroying their teeth because they eat products that contain large amounts of sugar. The new calorie–neutralizer diet teaches you the chemistry of foods and lets you substitute other tasty foods for the pies, cakes, cookies, ice cream and soft drinks that make you gain weight. In Chapter 8 learn how Virginia B. gained an incredible 60 pounds by overeating rich desserts and high-calorie foods. When she ate the calorie–neutralizer desserts (given in the same chapter) she satisfied her sweet tooth and at the same time continued to lose the entire 60 pounds in two months' time.

MAKE UP YOUR OWN REDUCING MENUS USING CALORIE–NEUTRALIZER FOODS

Now, as you begin to study and use the new calorie–neutralizer diet to lose your excess weight, realize that it is a flexible system in which you can choose your own foods and make up your own reducing menus to fit your exact requirements. You have a wide variety of meat, fruits and vegetables to select from. In fact, the fruits, vegetables and grains included in the new calorie–neutralizer diet will remove fat quickly because they take more calories to digest than they give in energy to your body. Chapter 4 gives two weeks of sample menus to use as a guideline for creating your own diet menus.

Anthony Norvell

FOREWORD

In my many years as a practicing physician and surgeon I have long been aware of the vital relationship between good nutrition and bodily health. Keeping a normal weight is a great asset to health.

I believe that one of the most thorough books on this subject is Anthony Norvell's latest book, *The New Calorie–Neutralizer Diet*. In this well-researched book, Norvell presents the accumulated knowledge of his years of study on the subjects of diet, nutrition and health. He believes that his dietary method is in keeping with the laws of nature and that it can help you maintain normal weight and good health. Norvell reveals for the first time in this outstanding book his new and original methods of achieving this objective for a lifetime.

Health-conscious Americans by the millions today are jogging, playing tennis, swimming, golfing and indulging in many other forms of exercise to keep in good physical condition. There is more interest today in health and diet than there has been for many years. Any book that helps achieve these high goals is worth reading. I believe that every person will benefit greatly by studying Norvell's book and applying the principles he suggests, for a sensible, quick weight-off diet.

Norvell is the author of 26 books on a wide variety of subjects. For many years he lectured in world-famous Carnegie Hall, and bronze plaques on the front of the Hall announced him as the 20th Century Philosopher. I believe this book is Norvell's crowning achievement as a lecturer and author, and I heartily recommend this work to anyone who is searching for a better way of life.

Harold Abrams, M.D., F.A.S.S.

Contents

**6. The Calorie–Neutralizer Foods That Supply
Valuable Vitamins While Reducing** . . . .

**7. The Calorie–Neutralizer Extension Diet
to Lose from 30 to 60 More Pounds** . . . .

Still Became 15 Pounds Overweight (127) . . . Use Wide
Variety of Vegetables While on This Variation Diet (128) . . .
Be a Vegetarian or a Meat-Eater—The Choice Is Yours (129)
. . . How to Spice Up Your Vegetables to Make Them
Delicious (129) . . .

Most Desserts Add Hundreds of Extra Calories to a Meal
(131) . . . She Gained 60 Pounds by Eating Too Many Rich
Desserts (132) . . . Henry J. Developed Symptoms of
Diabetes and Gained 90 Pounds By Overeating Sweets and
Carbohydrates (134) . . .

Use Raw Vegetables Whenever Possible for Salads (144)
. . . Salads Helped Della J. Lose 30 Pounds in Three Weeks
(146) . . . Excessive High-Calorie Salad Dressings Added
Weight (148) . . . Four Different Salads You Can Make from
Coleslaw (149) . . . More Hints on How to Give Your Taste
Buds an Extra Boost (156) . . .

Scientists Prove Foods Affect Efficiency and Sexual Activity
(159) . . . New Discovery: Lecithin Keeps Sexual Vigor at
High Levels (160) . . . Sexual Activity Also Stimulated by
Minerals in the Diet (161) . . . Obtain Important Minerals
Through Calorie–Neutralizer Foods (162) . . . Iron
Deficiency Made Her Constantly Fatigued (162) . . . Lack of
Manganese and 55 Pounds Overweight Caused Problems
(165) . . . Lack of Potassium Led to Chronic Constipation
(167) . . . Even When Your Weight Is Normal You Need
Vitamins and Minerals (167) . . .

The Food Gourmet Who Lost 65 Pounds (170) . . . Foods
Low in Calories Keep a Person from Being Hungry (174)

CHAPTER 1

The New Calorie–Neutralizer Diet That Can Work Miracles for You

In my many years of lecturing at world-famous Carnegie Hall as the 20th Century Philosopher, I traveled all over the world on a perpetual quest for a better way of life so that my thousands of students could have happy, healthy and prosperous lives.

Millions of Americans suffer weight problems that often bring on incapacitating mental and physical illnesses and cause premature death. Early in my career I realized that I must utilize my research to help people overcome the problem of excessive weight, which often leads to such serious ailments as high blood pressure, heart trouble, arthritis, diabetes, gall bladder disease, kidney disorders and many other forms of illness.

After many years of study and research in the fields of nutrition and biochemistry, I found out some amazing things about foods and the chemical mixtures that upset a person's normal metabolic processes, causing them to put on weight. These discoveries led to the formulation of my new calorie–

neutralizer diet for losing weight and maintaining the body in perfect health.

In my world-wide travels I visited various countries in the Near East and Far East. I saw people who were from 100 to 125 years of age, and they were still healthy, slender and active. Others, in their 70s and 80s, worked in the fields all day and were seldom ever fat. Their youthful appearance belied their years. I studied their life habits and their diets to discover the secrets of their good health and longevity. I found that they lived on certain easy-to-get foods, which they raised themselves. Natural, unprocessed vegetables, grains, fruits and nuts, with some milk products, formed the bulwark of their diet. They seldom ate meat, and usually it was in the form of fish and chicken. I later incorporated many of these natural foods in my new calorie–neutralizer diet for losing weight.

I also discovered that these sturdy people seldom ate in their daily diet the heavy starches and carbohydrates which are the mainstay of the American diet. Coincidentally, they also had few of the ailments which kill millions of people yearly in this country.

SCIENTIFIC FACTS BACK
THE NEW CALORIE–NEUTRALIZER DIET

There are some foods that act as catalysts, having the ability to change the chemistry of other foods when eaten in certain combinations. These calorie–neutralizer foods are mainly alkaline, helping the body reduce and eliminate the harmful acid ash that accumulates when acid-reaction foods are eaten. Alkaline foods consist mostly of high-fiber vegetables, fruits, nuts and grains. When combined with the highly acid foods, such as meat, sugars and carbohydrates, they change the nature of the fattening foods, causing them to be eliminated quickly from the digestive tract before they can be turned into fat cells.

For example, both beans and rice contain large amounts of carbohydrates, which are acid in reaction when eaten separately. However, when combined in the same meal, these two foods turn into valuable proteins and act as calorie–neutralizers, giving the body nourishment without adding fat cells or increasing weight.

Another important fact I learned about these calorie–neutralizer foods, which is really the secret of their ability to remove body fat quickly and safely, is this: Most of these fat-reducing foods take more calories to digest than they give to the body, so a person may eat up to 4 pounds a day of the calorie–neutralizer foods without ever gaining weight!

Some fruits, vegetables and grains are overbalanced in carbohydrates, which can cause a person who overeats them to become fat. In the new calorie–neutralizer program for quick weight loss I give a list of the heavy carbohydrate foods you should avoid if you want to lose weight quickly. When you have lost the pounds you wish, you can add other high-calorie foods to the lifetime sustaining diet to give you a normal, balanced and nutritional program that will keep you healthy and slender.

NATURE'S HIGH-FIBER
CALORIE–NEUTRALIZER REDUCING FOODS

In selecting the calorie–neutralizer vegetables, fruits and grains that help neutralize high-calorie fats and carbohydrates, I deliberately chose nature's own products that would resist quick digestion and absorption by the body. Most of these foods have a tough, high-fiber outer coating to protect them. When these fiber-rich vegetables, fruits and grains are taken into the human system, these outer fiber coatings resist the digestive processes and are hard to break down and assimilate. Some of these calorie–neutralizer vegetables are cabbage, string beans, asparagus, broccoli, cucumbers, tomatoes, spinach, green pepper, turnips and celery. These and other calorie–neutralizer foods furnish bulk in the intestinal tract. They give little or no nourishment to the body, but they do make you feel comfortably full at all times and they can never be converted into fat cells. These calorie–neutralizer vegetables also have a tendency to resist digestion when eaten in combination with calorie-rich foods, thus effectively neutralizing the effect that the high-calorie foods have on the body.

For example, lettuce appears soft and easy to digest, but it isn't. It has this fiber resistance and is one of the most difficult of all vegetables to digest. Corn also passes through the intestinal tract practically intact, resisting the digestive juices because of its protective, fiber coating.

There are also many fruits which take more energy to digest than they give to the body. These calorie–neutralizer fruits are in the alkaline reaction class. They neutralize the fat calories and dissolve the accumulations of acid ash that gather in the tissues and make you fat.

Some of these calorie–neutralizer fruits are: apples, cantaloupes, watermelons, strawberries, pumpkins, rhubarb, lemons, oranges and grapefruit.

All of the vegetables, fruits and grains included in the calorie–neutralizer lists are highly resistant to the digestive processes and delay the metabolizing and absorption of these foods. When eaten in combination with other rich foods, they tend to neutralize the high calorie content of these other foods, causing the body to eliminate them quickly, so they do not add fat cells.

WARNING! ALL FRUITS AND VEGETABLES ARE NOT CALORIE–NEUTRALIZERS

Despite the fact that most fruits are alkaline-reactive in their chemical effect on the body, they do not all fall into the category of calorie–neutralizers. Some are higher in carbohydrate content and should be avoided while dieting.

In the special reducing menus given in Chapter 4, you can eat as many as two or three calorie–neutralizer vegetables and fruits at any meal. They will help burn up the acid ash that has been deposited from acid-reaction foods like meats, potatoes, white bread, fish, chicken, pies, cakes and ice cream. You will be given some acid-reaction foods like milk, meat, fish, chicken and even butter, with many desserts, but at the same time in each meal the calorie–neutralizer foods you eat will help neutralize the rich calories such foods contain.

In priority list no. 1, I give the vegetables and fruits you are permitted to eat while reducing. The others in list no. 2 will be added to your diet later, if you have to lose from 30 to 100 more pounds. In this way you will be allowed a wider choice of reducing fruits and vegetables, although those in list no. 2 will not take weight off as quickly, for this reason: If you have to go beyond the usual two-week period to lose more than 30 pounds you want to be sure that you do not suffer the effects of quick weight loss, which might make you flabby.

CALORIE–NEUTRALIZER FOODS
ARE NATURAL SOURCES OF ENERGY

Nature, in her infinite wisdom, made the natural and nourishing foods easy to obtain in a plentiful supply of fruits, grains, vegetables and nuts. Meat was harder to obtain and long periods of time between hunts forced primitive man to depend on vegetables, fruits, nuts, berries and grains.

When civilized man began to refine nature's products, removing the essential nutrients like wheat and rice hulls to make white flour and white rice, mankind began a gradual decline in his state of health and fitness. Today millions of Americans are overweight and suffer from diseases attributed to obesity.

In the new calorie–neutralizer diet, you revert to nature's own balanced food plan, using the various combinations of vegetables, grains, fruits and nuts, with some meat, chicken and fish, to furnish a balanced diet.

A vast storehouse of natural sugars exists in dates, figs, apricots, grapes, bananas, oranges, pineapple and other fruits. They give the body sufficient amounts of natural sugars and essential carbohydrates for perfect nourishment, even when losing weight. You do not eliminate all fats and carbohydrates, even when reducing, for the body requires protein, fats and carbohydrates to be perfectly nourished. You control the amounts of fattening foods ingested, and reduce their impact by eating plenty of nonfattening, calorie–neutralizer foods, so your body does not put on extra pounds even when rich foods are eaten in the same meal.

When excessive amounts of foods are eaten and no effort is

made to reduce the caloric content, the body begins to store the extra calories as fat. The following case from my files illustrates the effects of such wrong eating habits.

FLORA G. OVERATE CARBOHYDRATES AND GAINED 48 POUNDS

When Flora G. came into my diet workshop to lose 48 excess pounds, she had tried three previous programs but they had not worked for her. She was consuming as many as 350 grams of carbohydrates a day and these rich calories were turning into fat. The normal amount of carbohydrates permitted in a day should not exceed 60 grams. I immediately put Flora on the calorie–neutralizer diet, but gave her such large quantities of nonfattening foods that she never really felt she was dieting.

Flora told me she had not been able to stay on any reducing diet, because she always felt starved, which forced her to sneak fattening foods into the diet. She occasionally went on binges of ice cream, cookies, pies, pizza or spaghetti. These high-calorie, carbohydrate foods were adding fat to her body with every bite.

In the very first week of the calorie–neutralizer diet, Flora lost 10 pounds. She never once complained of feeling hungry. Because she had all the vitamins and other elements she needed, she was never weak or lacking in energy. I gave her such a wide variety of meats, vegetables, salads, and fruits, that she did not feel the need of cheating on her diet and indulging her carbohydrate habit. In exactly five weeks from the day she started, Flora lost the entire 48 excessive pounds and felt marvelous.

YOU CAN EAT UP TO 4 POUNDS OF FOOD A DAY AND STILL LOSE WEIGHT

On this new calorie–neutralizer diet to lose weight, you can eat up to 4 pounds of food a day and as often as six meals a day and still lose from 8 to 12 pounds a week. You can eat many rich foods such as bacon and eggs, butter and real cream, and rich desserts twice a day, and still lose weight. This is because, along with these rich calorie foods, you will also be given enough of the calorie–neutralizer foods to offset any fattening effect they might otherwise have on your body. You will always feel completely full, as though eating normal meals, and never suffer from hunger pangs.

When you have lost your excess weight, whether it is 10 pounds or 100 pounds, you will then be given a modified, calorie–neutralizer sustaining food plan for the future, to keep you slender and healthy for the rest of your life.

Most reducing diets restrict the caloric intake from 900 to 1200 calories a day. In the new calorie–neutralizer diet you need not count calories, for the foods given in each day's menus are nonfattening and take more calories to digest than they give to the body. You can eat as many of these calorie–neutralizer foods as you wish until your appetite is satisfied, and never fear that you will gain an ounce! Later, you will be told when calories do count, and how to avoid foods heavy in calories.

CALORIE–NEUTRALIZER FOODS HELP MELT FAT AWAY

You can begin immediately to lose from 8 to 12 pounds a week on calorie–neutralizer foods. You will see the fat melt away as you add these low-calorie, nonfattening foods to your diet. They can be eaten in combination with lean beef, chicken and fish, and you will register a weight loss after only two or three days on this diet. Later I shall give you two full weeks of reducing menus that utilize these calorie–neutralizer foods. With such a wide variety of foods you will never become bored and want to stop your diet. You can even begin at once to make up your own menus.

Choose from the following list of calorie–neutralizer vegetables, eating at least two each day with your lunch or dinner. You can also eat them as often as you wish between meals whenever you feel hungry, and they will not add one single fat calorie to your food intake. In fact, the more of these calorie–neutralizers you eat, the more fat will melt away.

No. 1 PRIORITY LIST OF
CALORIE–NEUTRALIZER VEGETABLES

tomatoes	broccoli	okra
(fresh or canned)	turnips	spinach
cucumbers	green peppers	garlic
lettuce	mushrooms	asparagus
cabbage	watercress	radishes
cauliflower	leeks	Brussels sprouts
celery	string beans	

In the daily reducing menus I shall give later, you will find that these calorie–neutralizer vegetables are added each day to other foods, including lean meat, fish and chicken, so you will have a balanced, nutritious meal that gives you great satisfaction but which will begin to melt away the fat.

After the first week or two, if you wish to lose more than 10 to 25 pounds, you may add the following calorie–neutralizer vegetables to your menus for variety. They have more fat calories than those in the first list and they should be eaten more sparingly, possibly only one vegetable a day.

No. 2 LIST OF CALORIE–NEUTRALIZER VEGETABLES

beets	artichokes
carrots	peas
onions	red peppers
rutabagas	kale
squash	chives
parsnips	corn

HOW TO PREPARE THESE CALORIE–NEUTRALIZER
VEGETABLES

As most of the vegetables used in our reducing menus are the high-fiber variety, it is essential that they be prepared in a certain way to avoid destroying the fiber mass through over-cooking. Remember, these calorie–neutralizers are *not* intended to nourish the body and add fat. They are intended to neutralize the other foods you eat, which are high-caloried and contain fat, such as eggs, meats, butter, milk and yogurt. Most people cook their vegetables in water, losing many of their valuable elements and minerals. The best way to prepare these calorie–neutralizer vegetables is to steam them until they are soft enough to pass a fork through. You can then add a little margarine or butter for flavor. Some fat is needed each day, even when you are reducing, for the body requires at least two tablespoons of vegetable oil to metabolize the food you eat.

Eat as many of these vegetables as you can in salads, for when they are raw they retain their fiber bulk and perform their intended function better as calorie–neutralizers.

For example, cabbage is more valuable when it is eaten in the form of coleslaw than when it is cooked. It resists the digestive processes longer and is not easily absorbed. It also contains many valuable vitamins and minerals that are destroyed by cooking. Later I shall give several recipes for coleslaw that will keep this valuable food from becoming monotonous in your diet.

You can make tasty salads from raw vegetables such as cucumbers, green peppers, onions, radishes, spinach, mushrooms, watercress, lettuce and tomatoes. They will all help neutralize the calories that you eat in the main meat course of beef, chicken or fish. Avoid pork during the first two weeks of the diet as it has too many fat calories. You can also have in-between-meal snacks of celery, radishes, cucumbers and tomatoes without being afraid of overeating.

Add taste appeal to your calorie–neutralizer vegetables with spices, herbs and low-calorie dressings.

For some meals you can even include a baked potato with margarine. The starch in the baked potato will be offset by the calorie–neutralizer vegetables you eat in the same meal. Potatoes are 98 percent water and only add too many calories when fried in oil.

CALORIE–NEUTRALIZER FRUITS
YOU MAY EAT TO REDUCE

The following fruits all fall into the category of alkaline-reaction types and are extremely low in calories. They can be eaten in large quantities without adding weight. In fact, when you eat these fruits with any high-calorie meal, they will neutralize the absorption of the calories and keep them from adding fat cells to your body. Also, as these alkaline-reaction fruits quickly neutralize the acid ash contents of the body, they become a purifying and cleansing agent that keeps the body from becoming highly acid. An acid bloodstream is conducive to many forms of illness and upsets the metabolic balance of the body, causing it to absorb fat calories and store them in the intestines, stomach, hips and buttocks.

No. 1 PRIORITY LIST OF CALORIE–NEUTRALIZER FRUITS

cantaloupe	honeydew melon	strawberries
watermelon	rhubarb	lemons
apples	pumpkin	grapefruit
oranges		

These fruits are valuable as calorie–neutralizers because it takes more energy to digest them than they can give to the body, so they can be eaten in large quantities to appease your appetite without adding fat cells. For instance, if you are hungry, even after you have had a full meal, you can eat all the cantaloupe or watermelon you wish, or other fruits on this list, without being afraid of adding weight.

After the second week of dieting, if you wish to lose more than 20 pounds you can include calorie–neutralizer fruits from this second list. They are all in the alkaline-reaction category and you can eat them in small quantities to add variety to a prolonged period of dieting.

List No. 2 OF CALORIE–NEUTRALIZER FRUITS TO ADD LATER

peaches	limes	tangerines
apricots	pears	blackberries
nectarines	cherries	raspberries
pineapple	grapes	papaya
plums	prunes	loganberries

Remember that overeating the fruits in list no. 2 can give you too much natural sugar. Since carbohydrates in any form are fattening when overdone, these fruits should be eaten in small quantities and when it is necessary to stay on a reducing diet for more than one or two months to lose from 60 to 100 extra pounds.

LINDA A. LOST WEIGHT FIRST WEEK
THEN REGAINED IT SECOND WEEK

When Linda A. started on the calorie–neutralizer diet, the first week she lost 10 of the 20 pounds she was overweight. She was so pleased that she immediately switched to the no. 2 list of fruits and vegetables for her second week of dieting. She ate all she wanted of corn, carrots, peas and squash, as it was summer, and these were plentiful on the market. Then she included such fruits as peaches, plums, cherries and grapes, which were on the no. 2 list of fruits. She was shocked in the second week of her diet to find that she had lost only 3 pounds. She came to the diet workshop to ask why. When she admitted eating the forbidden fruits and vegetables in list no. 2, I knew the answer.

When Linda went back to the no. 1 list of fruits and vegetables for the next week she found that she easily and quickly lost the extra 7 pounds she needed to be her normal weight.

If you want to lose those extra 10 or 20 pounds quickly and easily, adhere to the no. 1 lists of calorie–neutralizer fruits and vegetables. If you have to lose from 30 to 100 pounds more, you must do it more slowly, and then you can include many of the fruits and vegetables in list no. 2.

AVOID CANNED FRUITS WHILE
ON THE CALORIE–NEUTRALIZER DIET

Most canned fruits are packed in heavy syrup, so they should not be eaten while trying to reduce. There are some dietetic fruits on the market that contain artificial sugar. These may be eaten if you do not have fresh fruits in the off-season months.

To lose from 10 to 30 pounds quickly on the new calorie–neutralizer diet you can begin immediately to eliminate the following carbohydrate foods that put weight on quickly. After you have lost the desired weight you may add some of these foods to your daily diet; however, you must never exceed 60 grams of the carbohydrate foods for the future or you will begin to rapidly put on the pounds that you have lost.

CARBOHYDRATE FOODS TO AVOID
WHILE ON CALORIE–NEUTRALIZER DIET

bananas
beans (except green
    or waxed beans)
candies of all types
cake
cashew nuts
chewing gum (with sugar)
cereals (except as given
    in daily menus, such as
    whole wheat and bran)
cookies
corn and corn products
cornstarch
crackers
white flour
white bread
dried fruits
dates
figs
honey
ice cream
jams and jellies

salad dressings (except those
    that are indicated)
sundaes and malts
hominy grits
white rice (brown rice is
    permitted)
popcorn
sodas
fried eggs
fried meats, fish and chicken
fatty soups
ketchup
spaghetti and macaroni
waffles and pancakes
sweet pickles
sweet potatoes
raisins
sweet relish
sugar and syrup
yams
yogurt

The above list is long and it may seem impossible to cut all these carbohydrates out of your diet for the few weeks you are on the calorie–neutralizer diet, but it is necessary to avoid them if you want quick, permanent results.

Even when you have lost the desired number of pounds, it is vitally important that you never return to eating large quantities of the above foods. Remember that fats have no carbohydrates, so you are permitted to eat some butter, mayonnaise, some salad and cooking oils, but only in small quantities. Most oils and meat fats are loaded with calories and in this instance, calories do count, for they are fat calories that are quickly digested and converted into body fat. If you eat more in one day than the body can use, these fats are stored in the body as unsightly fat.

SHE GAINED 40 POUNDS BY EATING TOO MANY FAT CALORIES

Doris T., who came into our diet workshop, was 24 years old. Her normal weight had been 125 pounds when she married five years before. She had two children in that time and after the birth of each child she developed a terrific craving for starches and sugars. Soon she weighed 165 pounds and felt sloppy. Her clothes no longer fit and her husband began to lose interest in her.

When I checked on her diet habits, I found that Doris ate doughnuts and coffee for breakfast, with cream and sugar. Cereals were eaten several times a week; she seldom cooked eggs or prepared any meat dishes for breakfast, such as ham or bacon. For lunch she usually ate a big hamburger on a roll, with French fried potatoes, and often a milkshake. She enjoyed heavy meat dinners, with mashed potatoes, gravy, and sometimes a vegetable, but always a rich dessert. Her husband was a construction worker and could handle as much as 3500 calories a day so he did not gain weight on this calorie-rich diet, but Doris could not handle it and her weight steadily increased.

The more of these rich carbohydrate foods Doris ate, the more she craved. She often sat before the TV set at night and stuffed herself on candies, popcorn, beer and pretzels.

The first thing I had Doris do was to eliminate most of these snack foods from her diet. Then she went on the calorie–neutralizer diet, eating as much as she wanted of all the permitted calorie–neutralizer vegetables and fruits, so she was never hungry while on the diet. She began to lose weight at the rate of 8 to 10 pounds a week. It took her six weeks to lose the extra 40 pounds, for she did not go on too stringent a diet, as I knew this would be bad for her psychologically. Soon she was back to her normal 125 pounds and felt fine, with no feelings of fatigue or boredom with her diet.

A WIDE VARIETY OF CALORIE–NEUTRALIZER FOODS PERMITTED

While you are on the calorie–neutralizer diet to lose weight you will be allowed to eat such a wide variety of foods that you will never feel deprived or hungry. You can eat bacon and eggs some mornings for breakfast; a wide variety of salads with low-calorie mayonnaise or special dressings for lunch; generous portions of steak, liver, hamburger (without bread, of course!) chicken, shrimps, crab, lobster, turkey and duck for dinner.

You can even include a tasty, sweet dessert at the end of your meals and continue to lose weight. Because you will have so many of the calorie–neutralizer foods intermingled with the calorie-rich foods, you will never feel that you are dieting. All the foods you will eat in the calorie–neutralizer diet will have more proteins, less fat and the minimum requirements of carbohydrates that are needed for good nutrition and health.

EVEN YOUR SWEET TOOTH WILL BE SATISFIED WHILE YOU LOSE WEIGHT

Right at the outset of your calorie–neutralizer diet you can begin to enjoy some tasty desserts. The following desserts are so low in carbohydrates that you can eat them in small quantities whenever you have an urge for sweets. In the case of melons you can eat all you wish for they take more calories to digest than they give to your body.

Jello (the type prepared with artificial sugar)
cherries
apples (stewed, baked or applesauce with artificial sugar)
raspberries or blueberries with milk
watermelon
cantaloupe
honeydew melon
peaches

banana custard, butterscotch junkets or chocolate (These are now on the market and a serving contains only about 40 calories.) pineapple (fresh, if possible, or canned in its own natural juices)

Avoid all sugar during the first two weeks of your diet and if you wish to sweeten coffee or other drinks, use artificial sugar.

In Chapter 8 you will be given many other low-calorie desserts that will satisfy your sweet tooth without adding weight.

SOME HINTS TO ADD INTEREST
TO FOODS WHILE DIETING

1. While you are on the new calorie–neutralizer diet to lose from 10 to 25 pounds, you should never feel that it is a difficult chore or that you are bored with the diet. Check out all the interesting fruits, vegetables and grains you are permitted on the reducing diet and utilize these to your benefit. This is especially important if you want to lose from 30 to 100 extra pounds, and must stay on the diet longer.

2. When you eat the calorie–neutralizer vegetables in salads, you can prepare a special type of dressing that is low in calories and still tasty. One such dressing can easily be made by mixing a little mayonnaise with ketchup, with a touch of apple cider vinegar. Even though mayonnaise is high in calories a small amount on your salads is permitted. There is also imitation mayonnaise on the market that has less oil and fewer calories. Chapter 9 gives some calorie–neutralizer salad dressings that you can use, not only while reducing, but later, to keep from ever again gaining weight.

3. In preparing some of the meats and other foods on the calorie–neutralizer diet, you can add a little cooking sherry to the sauces you put on your foods. Most of the alcohol evaporates, leaving only the flavor.

4. When preparing any of the calorie–neutralizer vegetables, you can add a touch of Worcestershire sauce or soybean sauce to the food to make it more appetizing.

5. You can keep between-meal snacks of high-protein,

calorie–neutralizer foods in the refrigerator and eat them whenever you feel hungry. These are mainly low-calorie foods that add no fat to the body. They can be leftover meats, hamburger, chicken, leg of lamb, liver or other meats from the previous evening's meal.

6. Whenever you feel hungry during the day, you can also eat small portions of cold shrimp, crab or lobster, with a low-calorie sauce. Slices of bologna, cheese and yogurt can be used as between-meal snacks. These foods should be eaten in moderation, but if you eat many of the calorie–neutralizer vegetables and fruits also, you can lessen their calorie content.

7. When you sit before the TV and are tempted to eat carbohydrate snacks such as potato chips, popcorn, corn products or beer, keep a tray of calorie–neutralizer relishes nearby and nibble on these. These can be cucumbers, radishes, celery stalks, tomatoes and lettuce. These can be eaten without dressing, and they will kill the appetite. If you insist on drinking soft drinks, make sure they are the dietetic kind without sugar.

CHAPTER 2

How to Reduce Harmful Acid Ash with Calorie–Neutralizer Alkaline Foods

Before you begin the actual reducing menus with the new calorie–neutralizer foods, it is important to know something about the chemistry of foods that can make you fat or keep you slender and healthy for life.

There are two categories of foods that make up the human diet. One is the acid-reaction type of food, which leads to obesity; the other is the alkaline-reaction type, which gives balance to the metabolism and helps remove the acid ash that accumulates from too many acid-reaction foods.

Here is why the new calorie–neutralizer diet is so effective for losing weight: Most of the fruits, vegetables and other foods used in the reducing menus fall into the alkaline-reaction category and the foods that are acid in reaction are used sparingly.

IMPORTANT FACTS YOU SHOULD KNOW
ABOUT YOUR BODY'S METABOLISM

In the past it was believed that one became overweight because he or she ate too much food. Overeating raised the caloric intake to a high level, causing the body to store the excess calories as fat.

Today it is a well-known fact that overeating is not the chief cause of obesity, although it is certainly a contributing cause. Most cases of being overweight are due to metabolic imbalance; that is, the body mechanism that burns up the food and turns it into energy and then into fat, in some way becomes unbalanced and is incapable of converting the food into energy. The body then stores the excess calories in the body as fat deposits.

If the body is fed 90 percent acid foods and only 10 percent alkaline, the balance is destroyed and the metabolism is affected. This causes the body to turn the ingested calories more quickly into fat tissues. If this balance of food is reversed and one eats 90 percent alkaline foods and only 10 percent acid foods, the body can more quickly neutralize the calories from the acid foods and keep them from becoming unsightly, unhealthy fat.

This is the secret of my new calorie–neutralizer diet. Most of the fruits, grains and vegetables used in the reducing menus fall into the alkaline category and the foods that are acid in reaction are used sparingly while dieting. When you have lost the desired pounds then this balance is changed, but you should never eat more than 25 percent acid-reaction foods, with at least a 75 percent intake of alkaline foods for a perfectly balanced normal diet.

MOST CARBOHYDRATE FOODS
ARE ACID-REACTION AND FATTENING

Almost all starches and sugars, which fall in the carbohydrate category of foods, happen to be acid-reaction in their effects on the body. When eaten in large amounts, meat also creates an acid effect on the body and must be balanced by the calorie–neutralizer alkaline-reaction type of foods for perfect metabolism. That is why in my reducing menus you will find there is meat at least once a day but it is used sparingly until you lose the weight you wish. For dieting purposes practically all carbohydrates are eliminated from the diet, with the minimum requirement of about 45 grams a day permitted. Later, when you have lost the required weight, this carbohydrate intake is raised to 60 grams a day, which is what the body requires for normal energy levels.

The typical fattening American dinner of meat, potatoes, white bread, gravy, and pie, cake or ice cream for dessert, is an unbalanced meal that can lead to obesity. When you consider the typical food eaten by millions of people today you can readily see why there are millions of overweight Americans. They consume tons of hot dogs, hamburgers, white bread, cookies and cakes, white rice, spaghetti, pizza, lasagna, ice cream and milkshakes. If these foods were eaten occasionally and offset by the calorie–neutralizers, they would not add excess fat to the body. The moment this typical diet is changed and the calorie–neutralizer foods are brought into a meal, the vicious carbohydrate habit is weakened and the metabolism immediately converts the acid foods into acceptable alkaline levels.

HOW TO BREAK THE CARBOHYDRATE HABIT

To break this insidious carbohydrate habit takes some willpower for the average person, but when you use the calorie–neutralizer diet it is easy to do, for you will no longer have a craving for the fattening, calorie-rich foods you formerly ate.

Most dieting systems insist that the reducing diet should contain 50 percent carbohydrates, 30 percent proteins and 20 percent fats. My research shows that overweight people who continue to eat up to 50 percent carbohydrate foods will never lose weight; in fact, they will continue putting on more weight. For example, if you were to eat one extra slice of white bread for one year you could gain as much as 15 pounds extra weight! Imagine what a lifetime of carbohydrate excesses can do to the average person.

You can begin immediately to break the carbohydrate habit by eating only the prescribed amounts given in the daily reducing menus found in Chapter 4. Avoid all the carbohydrate foods given in the long list in Chapter 1. You need not worry that you will not be getting any carbohydrates while you diet, for in the daily reducing menus you will receive enough carbohydrates from the calorie–neutralizer fruits, vegetables and grains that make up the daily menus.

IRENE S. BECAME 40 POUNDS OVERWEIGHT ON CARBOHYDRATE DIET

Irene S. was a typist in an office. She was 34 years old and weighed 40 pounds more than her normal 118 pounds. She had been steadily gaining weight for two years, and found herself going out less and less, having fewer dates and spending more time watching TV, usually while she munched on some carbohydrate foods.

In checking on her typical diet I found that Irene, without knowing it, had switched to high-calorie carbohydrate foods for most of her meals.

For breakfast Irene usually ate cereal with sugar and cream. A glass of orange juice and two cups of coffee with cream and sugar completed her meal.

Her office had a machine that dispensed soft drinks, candy bars and coffee. For her coffee break she would help herself to another cup of coffee with cream and sugar, and usually a chocolate bar to keep her from being hungry before lunch. For lunch she usually ate a hamburger on a roll, with a rich dressing, French fried potatoes and more coffee with cream and sugar. Sometimes she indulged herself and had a milkshake. Afternoon coffee break found her having a pastry with coffee and more sugar and cream. Another candy bar kept her from becoming hungry before dinner. She ate dinner alone, usually while watching TV, and sometimes it would be a prepared TVdinner, with potatoes, gravy and one small helping of a vegetable. These dinners included Swiss steak, chicken, turkey and roast beef, all served with potatoes and rich gravy. When she fixed her own dinners she usually had the powdered type of mashed potatoes, putting plenty of real butter in them, and sometimes a rich gravy. She ate desserts for each dinner, but seldom took time to prepare vegetables or salads. Once a week she might have a salad, but to make it tasty she loaded it with rich, high-calorie dressing. She bought a whole pie at the market when she shopped, and this often furnished her with desserts for several evenings. Sometimes she put a scoop of vanilla ice cream on the pie, and as usual, drank about two cups of coffee with cream and sugar.

Without knowing it, Irene was consuming as much as 400 or more grams of carbohydrates a day in this typical diet. This did not count the times she also snacked before bedtime, usually another calorie-rich dessert.

When Irene started her calorie–neutralizer diet to lose her 40 pounds, I realized we would have to begin slowly, to accustom her to the lowered carbohydrate intake. I permitted her to have some fruits and vegetables from both lists no. 1 and 2. In this way her weight loss was slower, but her hunger was appeased. She gradually shed the excess weight, although it took her six weeks to do so. Normally, on the no. 1 priority lists of calorie–neutralizer fruits and vegetables, it should have taken four weeks.

WIDE VARIETY OF FOODS PERMITTED WITH NEW CALORIE–NEUTRALIZER DIET

Now that you know the list of foods that should be avoided in your new calorie–neutralizer diet, you should also know the wide variety of foods that you can include in the daily menus. You need not actually bother counting calories if you are going to lose only 10 to 25 pounds, for this can easily be accomplished in two to three weeks but you should know the calorie content so you do not have to worry that you are going over the calorie count for quick reducing. This should be in the neighborhood of 1200 to 1800 calories per day. Each of these figures below is estimated for a generous portion of the food being served. Usually a serving of meat should be about 4 ounces per meal or approximately ¼ pound a day. Meat is included in the acid ash category of foods, but remember, the effects of acid foods in the reducing diet are offset by the alkaline content of the calorie-neutralizer foods that will also be included in each day's menu.

SELECT MEATS FROM THE FOLLOWING LOW-CALORIE LIST

	Calories
ground meat, without fat	215
sirloin steak	195
boiled or broiled beef	250
chuck steak, without fat	275
filet mignon	210
pot roast	200
T-bone steak	210
beef hearts	135
beef or lamb kidneys	225
beef or calf's liver	165
sweetbreads	205
tenderloin steak	240
lamb, without fat	200
lamb chops, broiled	165
lamb kidneys	115

HOW TO PREPARE LOW-CALORIE MEATS

While you are on this new calorie–neutralizer diet for quick weight-off, you should know how to prepare the low-calorie meats so that your body will get the proteins it needs without the excess fat. However, this little fat that does get into your reducing diet will not have harmful acid ash effects. It will not be absorbed by the body because of the high-fiber, calorie-neutralizer fruits, vegetables and grains that will also be included in each day's menus.

For the first two weeks you are on the new calorie–neutralizer diet you should eat at least 4 ounces of meat daily. This can be taken in the evening meal or at lunch, whichever you prefer. Meat should not be fried, (even when you are on a normal diet) for when you fry meat it has a tendency to soak in its own fat and becomes saturated. This is then absorbed by your body and adds fat calories.

Broil all meats; the fat drips down into the drain pan and can be discarded. Fried meats can increase the caloric intake by as much as 100 percent. Although you are allowed some sausage in breakfast menus, it should be the pre-cooked type that has most of the fat removed. You will be given enough fruits in the calorie–neutralizer list to neutralize the rich calories the breakfast may contain. Such tasty foods as bacon, ham, sausage and other meats are not eliminated entirely, for they satisfy the taste buds that have grown accustomed to these high-caloried foods over the years.

Do not baste the meats you broil, for that also adds to the absorption of fat. This includes fish and chicken. If the meat seems dry, pour a little water over it.

FISH: A SUPERIOR FORM OF PROTEIN TO MEAT

Fish has been found by nutritionists to be a superior form of protein to meat. You may prefer meat most of the time but include fish in your diet once or twice a week. You can replace meat with fish in any of the reducing menus given in Chapter 4.

There are low-calorie fish, as there are low-calorie meats, and later, I shall give a list of these so you can avoid the high-calorie meats and fishes. Select only those that are low. In my extensive studies of the Far-Eastern diets, I found that the health and stamina of many Orientals is because they eat a great deal of fish with brown rice and vegetables and very little red-blooded meat. As Japan and China are primarily agricultural countries, they are forced to substitute other forms of protein for meat. As a consequence you seldom see many fat people in these countries and they suffer less from high blood pressure and heart trouble than overly-fed Americans.

When you eat in a Japanese or Chinese restaurant in America you may observe that they serve many different types of vegetables and you can search in vain for a few pieces of pork, chicken or beef! Perhaps that is one reason why you may feel hungry again shortly after eating in an Oriental restaurant.

However, if more vegetables and other low-calorie neutralizing foods were eaten this feeling of hunger would not exist.

NEW CALORIE–NEUTRALIZER FOODS CONTRIBUTE TO LONGEVITY AMONG HUNZA AND TIBETAN TRIBES

It is also important to note that those Orientals who remain so slender and who live so long and have such enormous vitality, do eat many of the new calorie–neutralizer foods each day. These are in the form of whole-wheat, barley, brown rice (the hull is *not* removed from this food), lentils, oats and soybeans. These grains are all high in protein content with little fat. Many of these long-lived people grow their own vegetables, and of course they have their alkaline fruits such as oranges, lemons, limes, peaches, pears and the valuable apricot. Among the long-lived Tibetans and Hunzas, huge quantities of fresh apricots are eaten raw; the rest are dried in the sun and stored for winter use. This golden fruit, they claim, possesses amazing properties that give them good health and long life. You would probably consider the Hunza diet totally inadequate, consisting as it does mostly of fruits, vegetables, nuts, grains and dairy products, with little or no meat; yet these people are among the longest-lived in the world, some attaining the age of 135 to 145. Milk products are also included in the diets of these healthy tribes, with yogurt, cottage cheese and other cheese products used extensively. I also found that they ate the watery liquid that gathers on top of fermenting milk, called whey. This may be one of their dietary staples that adds to their amazing vitality and good health.

SOME DAIRY PRODUCTS INCLUDED IN THE NEW CALORIE–NEUTRALIZER DIET

For the first two or three weeks of the new calorie–neutralizer diet you will be given some dairy products. These should be used in moderation however, for whole milk contains fat. I encourage the eating of skimmed milk, some yogurt, cheeses and occasionally, real cream for coffee. It is preferable to receive your daily allotment of fats, necessary for perfect metabolization of foods, from milk products rather than meats. Corn oil, sunflower seed oil and other vegetable oils may be used sparingly.

If you fear high levels of cholesterol from drinking whole milk, you can use skimmed milk; in this way you can obtain extra proteins without cholesterol. Many doctors now believe that whole milk products create cholesterol in the blood that can lead to clogged arteries and various forms of illness.

Remember, fats in themselves do not turn into body fat, and some fats are needed by the body for perfect metabolizing of the foods you eat. Carbohydrates, including sugar and starch, are the foods that convert quickly into excess fat. Certain types of oil, such as olive oil and cooking oils made from animal fats, should also be avoided, for they are very high in calories and must eventually be turned into body fat.

While you are on the calorie–neutralizer diet, for the first two or three weeks you should also avoid all evaporated and canned milk, such as condensed milk, made with plenty of sugar. These are extremely high in calories.

A small amount of real cream may be taken on your cereals at breakfast and also in your morning coffee without danger of adding extra weight. However, all white sugar should be avoided and if you want coffee or tea sweetened, use the artificial sweeteners that are on the market. If you eat a slice of whole-wheat protein toast for breakfast you can use a teaspoonful of margarine and a half teaspoonful of marmalade on it.

STELLA B. WAS A MILK-A-HOLIC
WHO GAINED 30 POUNDS

When Stella B. came into my diet workshop to lose 30 excess pounds, she weighed 155 pounds; her normal weight was 125 pounds. Stella readily admitted that she had been a milk-a-holic for the past two years. She had a compulsion to drink milk and with it she consumed various types of cookies. Sometimes in the middle of the night she would awaken with a terrible craving for milk and sweets. She would often consume two glasses of milk at one sitting. At meals she used milk rather than coffee or tea. For breakfast she sometimes ate only bread and milk, but sometimes she varied this and prepared breakfast foods with plenty of milk and sugar. When she had coffee she used heavy evaporated milk, and for desserts she had custards and puddings that all required quantities of milk in their preparation.

However, I found that it wasn't milk alone that was making Stella fat; she cooked everything in olive oil. Her vegetables were drenched in olive oil; for salads, she used a special garlic dressing, in which the chopped garlic was allowed to sit in olive oil for several days before use.

On such a high-calorie diet, a person cannot help but gain weight. Milk products are permitted in the calorie–neutralizer diet, but they should be restricted and skimmed milk should be used instead.

Stella went on the calorie–neutralizer diet and lost 10 pounds the first week. She drank skimmed milk, and ate very few milk products. The second week she lost 12 pounds, and it was easy for her to lose the extra 8 pounds in the next week. Stella was warned that if she went back to her heavy milk drinking again, she would quickly put back the lost pounds.

In preparing the tasty salads which are included in the calorie–neutralizer menus, you should avoid olive oil entirely, because of its high caloric content. Use corn oil, which is lower in calories and unsaturated fats and without cholesterol. I have noted among the Latin races that use a great deal of olive oil on salads and for cooking, the fat they gain is of such a solid nature that it becomes almost impossible to remove it. This is one reason why you see so many overweight Latins when they reach middle or old age.

EAT CHEESE AND EGGS IN MODERATION ON CALORIE–NEUTRALIZER DIET

Too many cheese products contain excessive amounts of salt and should be eaten in moderation. Salt requires drinking large amounts of water. The body cells often retain this salt and liquid, giving a bloated appearance and adding body weight. I suggest that you use a salt product made from sea kelp or artificial salt, which can be found in most health food stores.

Eggs can be eaten in moderation in the calorie–neutralizer diet. Even though they contain high levels of cholesterol, the body needs some of this substance to line the arterial walls or the blood rushing through the veins and arteries would soon wear them out. The body manufactures cholesterol when it is not present in your diet. However, if you eat eggs sparingly you need never fear harm from them. The eggs should be boiled or poached, never fried. In some of the menus for breakfast I suggest omelets with various ingredients such as mushrooms, onions, ham, bacon, cheese, peppers, and other tasty products. In such instances the omelets may be made in teflon-lined pans that do not stick, or by using a product on the market which has no calories but which can be used for frying foods like eggs.

IMPORTANT FACTS YOU SHOULD KNOW
ABOUT SUGAR AND DIETING

No one should ever go on any reducing diet where he or she is constantly hungry. Hunger is nature's way of telling the body that food is required to keep the machine going. However, there is nothing in nature to tell you what kinds of food you should take to satisfy those hunger pangs, or to prevent you from overindulgence. This causes you to eat heavily of sugars and starches and other carbohydrates that are turned into fat quickly and stored on the hips, intestines and other fat-storing areas of the body.

Lowered blood sugar is the cause of hunger pangs. When the body's sugar supply drops dangerously low it flashes a signal to the brain for immediate relief. When this happens, and if the need for sugar is not satisfied, you experience fatigue, trembling and a feeling of weakness in the knees. Sugar depletion radically affects the brain and nervous system, causing you to act erractically. Your relationships with people can even become strained, causing you to act in a belligerent and hostile manner. Many people whose marriages break up often act under this type of strain.

Blood sugar does not mean sugar in the sense that we know it. Although when blood sugar is low you can eat a candy bar made with white sugar and it seems to give a quick pick-up in energy, this is a false energy and does not last. As soon as the effects of the candy wear off, there must then be more candy to continue the pick-up. When insulin is called forth to digest this excess sugar in the blood, the extra insulin continues to eliminate all other energy-giving elements in the blood. Finally the body is depleted of its insulin supply and is no longer able to create sufficient insulin to meet the body's ordinary needs. This extreme condition is called diabetes; its opposite, where there is too much insulin, is known as hypoglycemia. Either extreme, too much or too little sugar, brings an imbalance in the metabolic system that causes the glands to malfunction. This leads to the body's inability to handle carbohydrates, starches and sugars. The body then begins to store this excess sugar as fat, leading to serious weight problems as long as this condition exists.

An overweight person is constantly hungry because the blood sugar gets too high and the pancreas secretes insulin too fast; this results in the extra sugar in the bloodstream being removed too fast. Hunger is the body's signal of that need to replenish the body's sugar supply.

HER WEIGHT INCREASED FROM 125 TO 175 POUNDS IN TWO YEARS

Louise W. had a very severe case of blood sugar deficiency which caused her weight to increase from 125 to 175 pounds in two years. She was 32 years old, had two children and during both pregnancies she had a very strong desire for sweets. She'd heard that women often have unusual desires for food during pregnancies, so she thought it only natural that this should occur to her also.

Louise began to indulge her taste for sweets by eating cookies, cakes and candies. She often ate ice cream two times a day. Chocolates were her favorite candies; sometimes she would watch a soap opera during the day and consume an entire pound box of chocolates by herself!

In a short time, after eating the candy, Louise would feel highly exhilarated and have so much energy that she could finish her housework without effort. However, after an hour or two, she went into a tailspin and felt weak and highly tense, with periods of deep depression. Then she went to bed and stayed until her appetite drove her to seek out more sweets to satisfy her hunger pangs.

These cycles of renewed energy and deep depression were brought on by the body's need for more insulin to take care of the large quantities of sugar that had been dumped into the bloodstream. As the temporary energy she received from the candy wore off, Louise felt weak. This was relieved by eating more sweets, until the cycle brought her to a state of near-collapse.

One did not need to be a physician to diagnose Louise's condition. Her weight had increased to 175 pounds because of the heavy carbohydrates she included in her meals. Her cravings for high-calorie, fattening foods like spaghetti, mashed potatoes with gravy, pies and pizzas were the same as for sugar, for these carbohydrate foods are turned into sugar in the body and then converted into fat.

In following her calorie–neutralizer diet it was difficult for Louise to avoid all sugars and starches for the two months that it took her to lose 50 pounds. I did not rush her, because I realized that psychologically she was geared to these sweets, as an alcoholic is to liquor, so we used a somewhat slower approach to her weight problem.

Louise began to eat calorie–neutralizer vegetables and fruits from both lists no. 1 and 2. As cantaloupes and watermelons were then in season, we gave her all of them she could eat. When her craving for sweets was strong, Louise would eat as many as three cantaloupes between meals, and sometimes a quarter of a watermelon in the afternoon. This filled her up with nonfattening foods.

In the first month of her diet Louise lost 30 pounds. after that she slowly lost more weight, from 5 to 6 pounds a week, until at the end of the two months she was back to her normal weight of 125 pounds. Then Louise went on the lifetime sustaining diet, which gave her plenty of foods, including desserts, so she would never again go off on a fattening, carbohydrate kick.

METABOLISM CONVERTS FOODS YOU EAT INTO ENERGY

Your body's metabolism converts the foods you eat into the energy you need to work, play, make love and fulfill your life schedule efficiently and without great effort. In most young people this process is balanced and eats up the extra calories rapidly. When a person reaches the age of 35 or 40 the body's metabolism slows down and is not able to convert food into instant energy. It is then turned into body fat.

Each pound of fat contains about 3500 calories. A pat of butter has about 36 calories. If you eat just one extra pat of butter a day this will cause you to gain as much as 37 pounds in ten years! It is this accumulation of calories over the years that causes you to seemingly put on weight suddenly at 40 or 50 years of age.

In my new calorie–neutralizer diet you can begin immediately to shed from 10 to 25 pounds in the next two or three weeks by cutting out all carbohydrates and eating two or three of the calorie–neutralizer foods each day. Of course you will have some carbohydrates each day (this can hardly be avoided in the reducing menus you will use) but you will never have more than the 60 grams required to maintain good health and high energy. Most people take in as many as 450 grams of carbohydrates a day! All the excess calories above 60 grams of carbohydrates are turned into fat. This accounts for the fact that most Americans, who live on a high carbohydrate diet, put on extra weight after the age of 35.

Carbohydrates are found mainly in white bread, sugar, desserts, such as pies and cakes, ice cream and milkshakes, and in some vegetables. Meat, fish, and poultry, being protein, can be included in the calorie–neutralizer diet because they are not fattening, like the carbohydrate foods. However, even meat must be limited in the diet to about 4 ounces a day, for excessive eating of meat adds too many calories. These extra calories are harder to neutralize, even when you eat two or three calorie–neutralizer vegetables and fruits with a meal. When you have lost the required number of pounds, you can increase your meat, fish and poultry intake, without fearing the extra protein will be turned into excess fat.

Most of the vegetables used in the calorie–neutralizer reducing menus, given in Chapter 4, belong to the low-carbohydrate group. The second list of vegetables are higher in carbohydrate content and should be used only if your dieting is to continue for a period of one or two months to shed from 30 to 60 extra pounds.

USE ANY OF THESE LOW-CALORIE FISH

Add these low-calorie fish to your reducing menus at the beginning of your diet. This will give you a chance to get away from the monotony of meat each day. You can have shrimp, crab or lobster salad for lunch, with a calorie–neutralizer salad. Or you can serve any of the following fishes as a dinner dish, with two, warm calorie–neutralizer vegetables and a big salad with low-calorie dressing.

	Calories
salmon	80
tuna, fresh or canned in water	190
shrimp	125
raw oyster	60
flounder	80
sea bass	105
cod steak	100
abalone	120
shad roe	175

There are some dairy products which are in the low-calorie list that you may eat in small quantities while reducing.

Calories

cottage cheese	135
buttermilk	80
skimmed milk	50
evaporated milk	185
yogurt	85
whole milk	90

You can include the following poultry in your reducing diet for they fall in the low-calorie list.

Calories

turkey, without stuffing	200
broiled chicken	165
roasted chicken	215

As you go into the third and fourth week of your diet, if you must lose 25 to 100 additional pounds, you can avoid the monotony usually associated with dieting by shifting these foods around in your daily menus. The reducing menus will include one or two calorie–neutralizer foods in each day's menus so you need never worry that you are eating too much. They will not add more weight but will help dissolve the fat deposits, for they are in the nature of alkaline vegetables, fruits and grains that cannot add more weight to the body.

Knowing the caloric content of the above foods will help you keep within a reasonable range of 1200 to 1500 calories a day. However, this is not a rigid pattern in the new calorie–neutralizer diet, for even when you go up to 2000 calories a day the buffer foods will be eaten that neutralize those calories and keep them from turning into unwanted and unsightly fat.

Butter contains 920 calories in 4 ounces, so you can see why this rich fat must be avoided in any reducing plan. If you eat a little on toast you can counteract it with the calorie–neutralizer foods, but why take butter at all while reducing? Why not use a patty of margarine on your toast? A malted milk contains 510 calories, so you can see how quickly a malted milkshake and a hamburger for lunch can add up in high calories that make you fat. That innocent cream in your coffee, if taken three times a day with two cups at each meal, can add up to more calories than you should take for two or three days!

In the first two or three weeks of your reducing diet, exercise restraint in avoiding those foods that are high in calories. You simply cannot lose weight if you include them in your diet.

HIGH-CALORIE FOODS TO AVOID
IN YOUR REDUCING DIET

In the first two weeks of the reducing diet, avoid the following high-calorie foods completely. You should lose 10 to 15 pounds in a two-week period, depending on how rigidly you adhere to the calorie–neutralizer menus. If you must lose more weight you should still avoid most of these foods in the coming weeks. There will be exceptions, as when you are permitted to have a hamburger, made of lean meat, which has 390 calories per 4 ounces. But you will then be given one or two calorie–neutralizer foods at the same meal, thus lessening the caloric intake of that hamburger.

	Calories
frankfurter	305
Swiss steak	400
hamburger	390
tongue	340
cube steak	345
porterhouse steak	390
rib steak	325

AVOID THE FOLLOWING
HIGH-CALORIE POULTRY
IN FIRST TWO WEEKS

For quicker weight loss, especially in those crucial first two weeks, avoid eating the following high-calorie poultry. If your reducing diet continues beyond that two-week period, you may include some of these foods in your future menus, with suitable calorie–neutralizer foods to avoid putting on extra weight.

	Calories
chicken croquettes	370
chicken with dumplings	540
roast stuffed chicken	340
roast stuffed turkey	490

Avoid the following high-caloried fish in the first two weeks of your diet.

	Calories
fried shrimp	265
canned salmon	250
mackerel	295
fried oysters	275
sardines in oil	375
codfish cakes	245

ALCOHOLIC BEVERAGES ARE VERY HIGH IN CALORIES

If you have been used to imbibing alcoholic beverages before, with or after meals, you will find that these extra calories can add up quickly and keep you from ever losing weight. If you are really serious about losing weight, try to break this habit while you are dieting. Late in your sustaining diet you can take some forms of alcohol without putting on extra weight.

Following are the calories contained in 4 liquid ounces of the most popular alcoholic beverages.

	Calories
ale	75
beer	65
brandy	240
champagne	125
cognac	240
gin	310
rum	390
sherry	140
vermouth, dry	240
vermouth, sweet	240
vodka	310

	Calories
wine, dry	80
wine, sweet	135
whiskey	400

TOO MANY CARBOHYDRATES CREATE DANGEROUS ACID ASH AND ADD WEIGHT

When the diet is predominantly made up of acid-reaction foods such as meat, potatoes, white bread, sugar and cakes, pies and ice cream, the body builds large reserves of acid ash and quickly turns these high-caloried foods into excess fat. In order to bring about a balance between acid-reaction foods and those that are alkaline in reaction, you will be given plenty of calorie–neutralizer foods in each day's menu to help you avoid the problem of acidosis, which often comes when a person eats too many acid-reaction foods.

The following incident will explain what I mean.

Frank G. came into the diet workshop suffering from two obvious forms of dietary problems: First, he was 30 pounds overweight, and second, his doctor told him he suffered from a form of acidosis that would require medical care. When Frank's wife wrote out their typical menus for each day of the week I began to understand why he was overweight and why he suffered from acidosis. Frank's diet had been heavy in carbohydrates, sugars and starches. His wife, Mabel, did not suffer from being either overweight or from acidosis. That seemed strange until she revealed that she hated sweets, never ate bread, potatoes, cakes, pies or ice cream, which were items in Frank's daily diet. She served plenty of meat proteins and vegetables and frequently ate fruits, her chief source of desserts. Mabel's slender figure, compared to Frank's corpulent one, showed that his wife was eating a predominantly alkaline diet, while Frank was on a heavy acid-reaction diet.

We did not try to treat Frank's acidosis for we do not deal with medical problems in the diet workshop. However, we did put Frank on a very heavy alkaline diet, giving him two to three alkaline vegetables a day, which fell in the calorie–neutralizer category, and plenty of fruits that were alkaline in reaction, such as oranges, grapefruit and lemons. Apples and melons were also suggested. Frank was told to avoid all white bread, cakes, pies, ice cream, potatoes and other forms of carbohydrates.

Although meat protein is acid in reaction if eaten in large quantities, Frank was allowed to have generous portions of fish, chicken and steak or other forms of beef. To overcome the acid effects of this heavy protein diet, he was given alkaline vegetables and fruits that helped offset his heavy protein diet. For instance, green lima beans were given for some meals, as they are very heavy in alkaline reaction. He also ate lettuce and cucumbers with tomatoes for salads once a day, collard greens, turnip greens and turnips, which were alkaline in reaction, and fruits several times a day that helped neutralize the acid ash created by the proteins he ate.

All butter, milk and oils were removed from his diet for the first two weeks, except for a spoonful of corn oil a day, which he used with lemon juice for a salad dressing.

On this stringent calorie–neutralizer diet Frank lost 8 pounds the first week. This encouraged him so much that he easily kept on the diet two more weeks, when he lost 10 and 12 pounds more. But what amazed us most and also pleasantly surprised Frank's doctor was the fact that his acidosis disappeared completely after the second week of dieting!

CHAPTER 3

Nature's Fiber-Rich, Calorie–Neutralizer Foods That Melt Away Fat

In recent years, nutrition research has revealed some interesting facts about fiber-rich foods and their great value in any reducing diet. Most of these fiber-rich foods are in the calorie–neutralizer reducing diet. They neutralize the fat-producing elements that are in the average person's diet.

Most Americans eat a totally unbalanced diet, consisting of such high-calorie foods as hamburgers, milkshakes, white bread, potatoes, sugar, soft drinks, pie, spaghetti, pizza and lasagna, and ice cream or cake for dessert.

This type of diet produces tremendous amounts of acid ash in the body. This leads to an imbalanced metabolism that cannot handle the intake of acid-reaction foods, so it converts them into fat deposits.

There are certain combinations of vegetables and fruits that are so rich in fibers and alkaline in their reaction that they may safely be eaten in large quantities without fear of adding extra calories. These calorie–neutralizer fruits and vegetables stabilize the metabolism, causing it to function as nature intended, removing the fattening, high-calorie foods from the system quickly, before they can be converted into fat cells in the body. This speeding up of the metabolic processes also helps keep the system from absorbing extra rich calories that might be in the diet.

Before you begin the actual calorie–neutralizer diet to lose weight, you should know how the various calorie–neutralizer foods and their fat-dissolving elements work. I shall give a list of the fruits and vegetables in the reducing category and tell you how they affect your metabolism. In Chapter 4 I tell you how to include these calorie–neutralizers in your daily menus, so the fat will begin to disappear from your body the very first day of your diet. Even if your weight problem is as much as 50 to 100 extra pounds, you will be given an extension diet that will add other calorie–neutralizers to your daily reducing menus for quick weight loss.

CRAVING FOR CARBOHYDRATES
MADE LOLA D. 32 POUNDS OVERWEIGHT

There is a great difference between fat calories and those that do not add weight. Most carbohydrates are definitely in the fat-calorie category and quickly add weight. A case in point was that of Lola D., who came into my calorie–neutralizer diet workshop with a distressing problem. She was 24 years old, single and 32 pounds overweight. As she was only five feet one inch in height, this condition caused her to look unshapely and she felt that men were not attracted to her. There were no physical illnesses and her main concern was to lose weight to improve her love life.

Upon checking her eating habits I found that she was a carbohydrate addict, constantly nibbling on fat-calorie foods. She ate candy while watching TV every night. She kept a big cookie jar filled with delicious cakes and cookies, which she ate between meals. She kept ice cream stocked in her freezer and had a big dish of it every night for dessert. Finally, when her clothes no longer fit her and she was all out of shape, she found herself forced to do something.

Lola was gradually given the withdrawal treatment from her carbohydrate addiction. At first it was painful and she cheated on her calorie–neutralizer diet the first two weeks. She conquered her fat-calorie habit by substituting the calorie–neutralizer fruits and vegetables for sweets and soon began to lose weight. The results were not dramatic at first, because those masses of fat cells screamed for fat foods. When fat cells gain a stronghold in the body they want to continue to thrive and live and reproduce more fat cells. They do not like to be killed off, and this brings about a struggle between the will to live and the will to die, until either the fat cells win out or the body claims its right to life and liberty, free of clumps of ugly, sickly fat.

In Lola's case she lost only 5 pounds in the first week. In her second week on the calorie–neutralizer diet, as she ate more and more of the low-calorie vegetables and fruits, she lost 10 pounds. This so encouraged her that it was simple from then on to lose the other 17 pounds. Five weeks from the day she began her diet, Lola had lost the full 32 pounds and her hips, thighs and breasts were back to a normal and attractive size.

This story has a happy ending: Enrolled in the diet workshop at the same time with Lola was a young accountant who was 40 pounds overweight. When they got together and compared notes on their progress they found they had so much in common that they fell in love and became engaged!

THE FOLLOWING CALORIE–NEUTRALIZER VEGETABLES RESIST CALORIE ABSORPTION AND MELT AWAY FAT

The following calorie–neutralizer vegetables belong in our priority no. 1 list. You can include two or more of these in each day's menus. These vegetables all have high fiber content, give bulk to the digestive tract, and resist calorie absorption. They should be used for the first two weeks of your diet for quick weight loss. These vegetables are also alkaline in their chemical reaction, not acid, thus avoiding the accumulation of harmful acid ash in the body's cells.

Cabbage

Cabbage is high on the list of foods that add fiber. It is an excellent calorie–neutralizer. This valuable food may be eaten raw in coleslaw, or steamed until tender and eaten with margarine, a little butter or some low-calorie sauce.

Later, I shall give several recipes for making coleslaw that will help add variety to your diet. Cabbage is high in sulfur content, making it an excellent brain food. Cabbage is a cleanser, adds roughage to the intestinal tract and is a good buffer food to help avoid the absorption of calories that might be ingested in the same meal.

Carrots

Although carrots belong to the second category of calorie–neutralizer foods, you can begin to use them in the first week of your diet, if they are combined with other low-calorie vegetables such as cabbage, cauliflower or asparagus. Carrots are also high in vitamin A, which is essential for bone formation, good digestion and proper functioning of the respiratory tract. This important food is also thought to help in avoiding premature aging and to add extra years to life. Lack of vitamin A drastically affects your metabolism, causing it to quickly form fat deposits from the food eaten.

Tomatoes

One of the most valuable calorie–neutralizer foods you can eat while losing weight is tomatoes. You can eat as many tomatoes as you wish, with their skins on for fiber, and raw, in salads or canned, when you cannot obtain them fresh.

For a variation, when you have to lose more than 20 pounds you can even go one whole week on various types of meat proteins and tomatoes, without having any other calorie–neutralizers. Your weight will continue to melt away. This is because the tomatoes are highly alkaline in their reaction and burn away the acid ash more quickly than other vegetables. You can even include meat, fish or chicken in your daily diet twice a day, if you eat tomatoes with the food. You can have snacks of tomatoes, celery, radishes and cucumbers between meals. These high, calorie–neutralizer vegetables will keep your body from absorbing the extra calories that the large quantities of meat supply. On the calorie–neutralizer diet you can stray from any rigid diet plan and formulate your own plan, one that gives your taste buds satisfaction, and still continues to melt the fat pounds away. Tomatoes are also high in vitamin C and contain many other valuable elements the body needs.

Spinach

Here is a vegetable that has high priority on the calorie–neutralizer list of foods. It does not add fat calories to the diet and can be eaten raw in salads, with low-calorie dressings, or cooked, for its bulk and fiber content. You can fortify any high-protein meat meal with spinach and be assured that its slow-digesting, high-fiber nature will rapidly neutralize any fat calories you may have taken at that particular meal. It is also rich in minerals and vitamins.

Celery

Celery is an appetite killer, an excellent calorie–neutralizer, with a high fiber content. These three things make it a valuable vegetable to add to your reducing diet.

Celery can be eaten raw or cooked. It has a high calcium content, as well as sodium, which the body needs. This takes the place of forbidden salt (sodium chloride), which is a poison. If you must have salt, try using the forms of ground sea kelp and seaweeds featured in health food stores. Sodium can be furnished to your body in fresh celery, radishes, cucumbers and tomatoes, as well as other fresh vegetables. Keep these in your refrigerator while dieting and whenever you are hungry you can eat these valuable vegetables between meals.

Cucumbers

Cucumbers are low in calories, high in fiber and very valuable as a calorie–neutralizer food. Eat cucumbers sliced, skin and all, with a tomato and lettuce salad, and a low-calorie dressing.

Have as many as you want. They will help neutralize the calories furnished by other foods in your meal and keep you from putting on extra fat.

Lettuce

Lettuce furnishes your digestive tract with a highly-rated fiber and calorie–neutralizer that works your digestive tract overtime, using up calories that would otherwise turn into fat.

Lettuce is one of the most difficult of all vegetables to digest. Because of this, the metabolic processes are slowed down, eliminating the high-calorie foods without adding fat to the body. You can eat all varieties of lettuce, as they all possess the same calorie–neutralizer value.

Mushrooms

This is one of nature's most valuable calorie–neutralizer foods. Mushrooms can be eaten raw, in salads, or made into delicious dishes. They are tasty and give few calories. Later I shall give recipes for using this calorie–neutralizer vegetable in appetizing dishes, soups and salads.

Asparagus

The bulk and fiber to be found in asparagus, as well as its calorie–neutralizer value, makes it a choice vegetable to use in your reducing diet. Eat fresh asparagus in salads, or use it as a side dish with any meat, chicken or fish course. Prepare by steaming it until soft; then add butter or margarine for flavor.

String Beans or Wax Beans

String beans can be used in cooking delicious meat dishes, or prepared solely as a vegetable, with tomatoes, garlic and a little vegetable oil. The few extra calories furnished by the oil do no harm, as the bulk and fiber of the string beans will keep the body from absorbing any food value. String beans can also be combined with other vegetables in a big salad, such as cauliflower, green peppers, lettuce, cucumbers, and watercress. A tasty low-calorie salad dressing can be added that makes such a salad delicious. The main value of string beans, however, is in furnishing the body with enough calorie–neutralizers to completely block the digestive track from absorbing the calories in any meat meal where you eat carbohydrates or sugars for dessert.

Turnips

The sturdy turnip, the white variety or the rough cream-colored rutabaga, is extremely valuable because it is such a low calorie–neutralizer. You can eat until full of this vegetable, and it adds nothing fattening to your body.

Brussels Sprouts

Cook Brussels sprouts until soft enough to pass a fork through, and flavor with margarine or butter. This vegetable is a fine calorie–neutralizer and adds bulk without adding calories.

Green Peppers

Green peppers are high in vitamin C but this calorie–neutralizer vegetable is valuable for other reasons. It is an alkaline-reaction type that helps reduce excess acid ash. It can be used raw in salads, or fried in oil. Vegetable oil is preferred to olive oil. The little oil you use in cooking will not be turned into fat, for remember, fat is not a carbohydrate. It is the starch and carbohydrates in a diet that turn into fat deposits on the body. You require at least two tablespoons of some form of vegetable oil each day for maintaining proper metabolism. Without some oil the body mechanism does not work properly.

The most important thing to remember about all of the vegetables given above is that they require more energy to digest than they give to the body. No matter how many of these you eat, or in what combination with other foods, they cannot make you fat. By making the metabolism work harder to digest these calorie–neutralizer vegetables, you use up any extra calories that are in your diet. In fact, this extra work for the digestive tract will take so many calories to digest these fiber-rich vegetables, that they will work to reduce any caloric intake from other foods eaten at the same meal.

The following case from my diet workshop files shows how a diet lacking in salads and vegetables caused one person to gain 50 pounds.

THE ILLUMINATING 20-POUND TURKEY

It took a holiday bird for Fred S. to realize he was tired of carrying around 50 pounds of excess body weight.

A few days before Thanksgiving, Fred's wife sent him to the market to buy a 20-pound turkey for their dinner. Fred became so tired carrying it the four blocks to where they lived that he had to stop twice to rest before continuing.

Fred began to reason: If a 20-pound turkey could make someone so tired in such a short time of carrying it, how much more tired that person would be from carrying the equivalent of a 50-pound turkey in fat deposits on his body! That moment of illumination helped Fred make his decision to try the calorie–neutralizer diet to lose his excess weight.

Fred had always been a heavy meat and potato eater, with good old-fashioned pies for dessert. His mother brought him up on this diet and seldom prepared vegetables or salads for dinner, so he grew up with a craving for heavy proteins and rich carbohydrates. He had been pudgy as a boy and thought it ran in the family as his mother was heavy and his father was always from 50 to 60 pounds overweight. His father died at the age of 56 from a heart attack, but at that time no one associated it with excess weight.

Fortunately, Fred's wife, who was also 25 pounds overweight, came into the workshop with her husband to lose her extra weight. They both began to eat the many tasty calorie–neutralizer vegetables given in this list. Helped by plenty of protein and some carbohydrates, they found the fat melting away until each had returned to normal weight. At each meal they had at least two of the calorie–neutralizer vegetables, with a big salad of raw vegetables. Their desserts were mainly fruits in season and low-calorie puddings and custards. They snacked on relishes such as cucumbers, celery stalks, tomatoes, radishes and carrots.

Not only did Fred lose his 50 pounds but his health so improved that his doctor found his blood pressure normal. His high blood sugar, which could turn into diabetes, subsided. His wife lost the entire 25 pounds in three weeks time. Both of them went on the calorie–neutralizer sustaining diet which would assure them of never again becoming overweight. That diet is given in Chapter 12.

EAT THESE CALORIE–NEUTRALIZER FRUITS AT ANY MEAL

Let me emphasize: You can use any of the fruits on the no. 1 priority list, eating them as often as you wish during the day, between meals and with meals. These calorie–neutralizer fruits take more energy to digest than they give to the body, so they can never add weight.

These calorie–neutralizer fruits can be eaten as desserts or made up into tasty fruit salads, using a low-calorie dressing of sour cream, yogurt or low-calorie mayonnaise.

cantaloupes	lemons
watermelons	apples (cooked or raw with peeling)
honeydew melons	rhubarb (sweeten with artificial sugar)
strawberries	pumpkins
oranges	grapefruit

After the second week of dieting, if you are trying to lose from 25 to 100 more pounds, you can gradually expand this list to include all of the fruits given in list no. 2 of the calorie–neutralizer fruits. Remember, eat sparingly of these, for they are higher in calories than those in list no. 1, but they add variety to the desserts and give you the feeling you are not dieting.

Cantaloupe

This delicious calorie–neutralizer fruit has many valuable vitamins and minerals, including vitamin C. It can be eaten between meals, before meals, or after, as a dessert. Cantaloupes

act in an alkaline manner; they tend to flush out the accumulations of acid ash and keep you from putting on extra weight.

Watermelon

Watermelon is another valuable calorie–neutralizer fruit
which can be eaten in season as often as you wish. It acts as a
catalyst, is alkaline in reaction, and has no carbohydrates, no
cholesterol, no fat, making it the ideal reducing fruit. When in
season use it as often as you wish to assuage hunger pangs, and
to give you valuable minerals and vitamins.

Strawberries

You can usually obtain strawberries year-round, but if you
cannot, they can be bought frozen and used for tasty desserts or
eaten with a little cream. Strawberries do not add extra calories
and tend to neutralize the fat calories from other foods in a meal,
so they can be eaten as a dessert when you have a rich protein
meal.

Summer is probably the best time to go on a reducing diet,
especially the calorie–neutralizer diet, for it is then that most of
the fruits and vegetables are readily available.

SARA M. WAS ONLY 28
WHEN HER WEIGHT INCREASED 32 POUNDS

When Sara M. first began to gain weight she attributed it to
the fact that weight ran in the family. Her parents were both
overweight and had been for as long as Sara could remember. As
she was single and dating a fine young man who seemed serious, Sara was sure that he accepted her, weight and all, as she
was. She did not worry too much as her weight increased until
she was 32 pounds overweight.

It was only when her boy friend mysteriously stopped
taking her to dances and parties that she began to wonder if it
could be because she was getting too fat and unattractive? One
day a man passed her on the street and winked at her, saying at
the same time, "Hi, chubby!" He stopped, seeming to want to

talk to her, but she fled in panic at the word "chubby." Sara knew she had to do something to overcome her weight problem.

It was in August of that year that Sara came to our diet workshop and told me her story. She confessed that of late her appetite had grown tremendously and she craved food more than ever before. I knew that her romantic frustrations were causing her to substitute food for love. Her desire for sweet, carbohydrate foods made her eat up to as many as 400 grams a day of candies, pies, cakes and ice cream, with less meat and vegetables.

When Sara began the calorie–neutralizer diet and saw the menus she was to use for the next three weeks, she confided to me, "I could eat three times more than you give us in these menus." That might have been an exaggeration, but I knew what she meant: Sara felt that she was being denied the carbo-hydrate goodies she had grown accustomed to eating, and this proved to be a big challenge for her.

When I told her she could eat cantaloupes four times a day, and all the watermelon, strawberries and other vegetables in the no. 1 list, she felt somewhat better. In the second week of her diet, I added some of the fruits and desserts that were higher in carbohydrates, so she would not get off the diet.

It took Sara a little longer than the three weeks that it usually takes to lose 20 to 35 pounds, because she crammed low-calorie fruits between meals, with meals and again at bed-time.

By using the calorie–neutralizer diet, she lost the excess weight easily and without any psychological blocks. Soon she was down to her normal weight and dating once again, so, for Sara, the effort to lose weight had been worthwhile.

Apples

The old saying, "an apple a day keeps the doctor away" is based on fairly good logic. This fruit is one of nature's fine aids in maintaining good health. Eating two or three apples a day cer-tainly aids regularity and this, in turn, keeps the body function-ing properly. But the apple's greatest value as a high-fiber, calorie–neutralizer fruit is as an aid in keeping the harmful acid ash at a low level and delaying the absorption of extra calories from other foods.

Apples may be eaten raw, with the skin, or you can stew them with a little honey, or make applesauce of them, eating it as a dessert as often as you wish. Baked apples are also a good form of dessert. You can make a custard and mix the stewed or baked apples for a filling and delicious dessert.

Rhubarb

This high-fiber fruit is an excellent calorie–neutralizer. It acts as an alkaline and at the same time satisfies the taste buds for something tangy. It can be prepared with artificial sugar to avoid the calories of white sugar or honey. A rhubarb pie can be made with whole-wheat flour or you can make rhubarb tarts to eat as a dessert as between-meal snacks with tea or coffee.

Oranges

This is an excellent calorie–neutralizer fruit and also a good source of vitamin C, which should be taken every day in some fruit or vegetable to furnish the supply needed daily. While you are reducing it is not wise to drink the usual 10-ounce glass of orange juice recommended. All juices are absorbed quickly by the digestive track and, as they are usually high in sugars, they can turn into fat quickly if you drink too much. It is better to eat the pulp of the orange after skinning it. In this way you utilize the calorie–neutralizer, high-fiber content of this valuable fruit.

Lemons

The same thing can be said about the lemon for obtaining daily requirements of vitamin C. Half an hour before breakfast, squeeze the juice of a whole lemon in a glass of water and drink it. It should not be sweetened but drunk plain, for the best effect. It is a great aid in flushing out acid ash from the body cells, is high in vitamin C and is an alkaline-reaction fruit even though it is in the category of citrus acids, the same as oranges, grapefruit and limes. Do not overdo drinking orange juice, lemon or grapefruit juice, for you must maintain a balance between alkaline and acid in the bloodstream to have good health. A person who is overly acid develops acidosis, and one who is overly alkaline also destroys the body's delicate balance.

Pumpkin

This fruit can act as a calorie–neutralizer and at the same time furnish your body with valuable vitamins and minerals. It is not fattening in itself, but if you make it into a pie, adding milk, eggs and white flour, it is instantly changed and becomes rich in calories. Eat the pumpkin as you would summer squash, steamed or cooked until soft, adding a little artificial sweetener. If you wish to make it into a pie or tarts, use whole-wheat pie crust and avoid enriching it with eggs or milk or butter.

Grapefruit

This fruit falls into the same calorie–neutralizer category as oranges and lemons, and should be eaten with the pulp, before breakfast, or any time during the day when hungry. It is a good appetite killer and also contains vitamin C and other essential minerals and elements.

YOU CAN ADD SOME GRAINS TO
YOUR LIST OF CALORIE–NEUTRALIZERS

Despite the fact that grains and legumes are considered to be carbohydrates, you can include some grains and such legumes as lentils and beans in your reducing diet without fearing they will add weight. It is unwise to eat as much as 50 percent carbohydrates in a reducing diet, for you cannot lose weight with such a heavy intake of starches, sugars and oils. If you eat some grains and add one or two calorie–neutralizer fruits or vegetables to the meal you can safely include cereals for breakfast, whole-wheat toast, and occasionally cornflakes, whole bran, oatmeal and cream of wheat products. You can even eat these with real cream, for cream contains fewer carbohydrates than whole milk. If you use artificial sugar on these cereals you can safely add them to your reducing menus.

You can also occasionally have brown rice, served with two of the calorie–neutralizer vegetables, and 4 ounces of protein meat, without having to worry about adding extra calories or starch. In fact, if you eat baked beans and brown rice at the same meal, they act as catalysts and chemically change the nature of both from starch to protein! Many people substitute beans and rice for meat, obtaining the needed proteins from these two grains.

In planning your reducing menus, in addition to those which I give in Chapter 4, you may add any of these cereals for your breakfast meals or as adjuncts to your protein meat dishes. They will give a wide variety to your reducing menus and satisfy the hunger urge for some carbohydrates. Also, remember, you are allowed up to 45 grams of carbohydrates a day in the calorie–neutralizer diet for reducing. By adding some of these grains and legumes to your daily menus you will be filling this requirement.

Navy Beans

Beans are predominantly starchy and therefore they fall into the carbohydrate category. However, there is also a heavy protein content in these valuable vegetables so you may include them in your reducing diet occasionally. Baked beans can be eaten once a week, or you can make a bean soup that fills you without endangering your diet in any way.

Lentils

The same thing holds true for this legume as for the navy beans. Cooked with chopped onion, a little oil, and a spoonful of tomato paste, lentils make a delicious noontime repast. You can add some cut-up frankfurters to the lentils for extra protein. Be sure you also serve a salad made up of raw, calorie–neutralizer vegetables with the lunch or dinner, and you can also add a fruit compote for dessert, made up of calorie–neutralizer fruits. This will assure you of not absorbing the extra carbohydrates you obtain from the beans or lentils.

Whole-Wheat Grain

Whole-wheat grains, as well as barley, oats, soybeans and brown rice are all in the carbohydrate category of foods. You can use these for varying your reducing menus by having whole-wheat toast for breakfast, whole-wheat cereals, such as whole bran, and other cereals that are made of wheat or corn products. Eat only small portions of these grains, and use artificial sugar and real cream. Before such a carbohydrate breakfast you may have a whole orange, eating the pulp as well as the juice, or half a grapefruit, or a dish of strawberries, rhubarb, or any other of the fruits in the calorie–neutralizer no. 1 priority list.

Oatmeal is a vital food with sustaining qualities that make it excellent as a breakfast food. Cream of wheat is a heavy starch but if you eat only a small portion occasionally for breakfast it cannot do any harm. If you obtain the whole-wheat types of cereals, including bran products, you can safely add variety to your breakfast menus, and still lose weight safely and easily. It is only when you eat these starchy products without adding the calorie–neutralizer fruits and vegetables that you will begin to add many unnecessary fat calories. Calorie–neutralizers help rush these foods through the intestines before they are absorbed as fat calories into the bloodstream.

CHAPTER 4

Start Your Calorie–Neutralizer Reducing with These Two Weeks of Delicious Menus

Now that you understand the basic facts about the new calorie–neutralizer foods and how to use them, you are ready to begin your first two weeks of dieting to lose from 8 to 12 pounds a week. If you wish to lose 25 or more pounds, you can extend these menus, with variations that I shall give, so that the fat will continue to disappear as long as you wish.

You are not limited to these menus however, for now that you know our basic calorie–neutralizer foods you can make up your own menus, drawing from the lists of vegetables, fruits and grains that are permitted. You even can have a wide selection of meats by using the lists given and choosing those that you prefer for any given meal.

In each day's menus you will be given delicious reducing foods, with the calorie–neutralizers spaced for each day so you do not need to worry about overeating too many high-calorie foods in any one meal. For example, on the second day's lunch menu you will be given fresh vegetables in sour cream. You may wonder if sour cream is high in calories, as it has a high fat content. However the calories in the sour cream are neutralized by the cucumbers, green onions, radishes, green peppers, tomatoes and celery stalks used in the salad. These are all calorie-neutralizer vegetables and protect your body from the high-caloried sour cream you used. If you ate the sour cream alone, without the calorie–neutralizer vegetables, you would almost certainly add weight.

For some breakfasts you will be given bacon and eggs, eggs Benedict with Canadian bacon, cereals, creamed tuna on whole-wheat toast or a Cheddar-cheese omelet. You may think that such a heavy breakfast will almost certainly be turned into fat cells, but you will be wrong. At the same meal you will be given calorie–neutralizer foods that keep your body from absorbing the high calories and fatty foods.

An important factor in the new calorie–neutralizer diet is that you will eat enough foods each meal so you feel comfortably full at all times, as well as being perfectly nourished.

If you include little extras each day that are high in sugar content, without taking extra calorie–neutralizer foods to counteract them, you will almost certainly never lose weight.

JEANNE L. STRAYED FROM CALORIE–NEUTRALIZER DIET AND GAINED WEIGHT

When Jeanne L. was young she felt she would never be one to gain weight and have to reduce. However, when she reached the age of 25 and had a one-year-old son, she began putting on extra weight. She did nothing about it until she noticed that she was having difficulty getting into her dresses, which had somehow mysteriously shrunk. By this time Jeanne was 150 pounds; her weight when she had married was 110.

In checking Jeanne's daily diet I found that she was not overeating carbohydrates and her meat intake was normal, with some salads and occasional vegetables. However, she admitted that several times during the day, whenever she became thirsty, she would drink a favorite soft drink filled with sugar. Some days she consumed as many as four bottles.

She usually ate two fried eggs with bacon, and had two or three pieces of white toast with butter and marmalade. She added cream and sugar to her two cups of coffee, giving her an excessive amount of carbohydrates.

Jeanne did not realize that these seemingly trivial dietary habits were giving her excessive amounts of carbohydrates and gradually they were being converted into fat deposits on her body.

I did not remove the soft drinks from her diet, but suggested she try the diet drinks on the market. She eliminated all white bread and ate one slice of whole-wheat or protein bread with a little butter and low-calorie marmalade. She retained the cream in her coffee, as she needed some fat even in the reducing diet, but used artificial sugar.

Jeanne began to eat two or three calorie–neutralizer fruits and vegetables with her lunch and dinner. Throughout the day snacks were permitted of different vegetables and fruits so she would not feel hungry at any time.

Jeanne stuck with her diet this time; she lost 10 pounds the first week and an additional 7 to 8 pounds in the following weeks. When she had shed the entire 40 pounds she went on the sustaining diet, given later, and retained her normal weight without further difficulty.

FIRST WEEK MENUS

FIRST DAY

Breakfast: Two eggs, poached, boiled or fried in margarine.
Three strips of bacon, crisp, fat fried out.
One slice of whole-wheat toast with real butter or margarine and a spoonful of marmalade or jelly.
Coffee, tea, with real cream and artificial sugar.
Calorie–neutralizer fruit: one-half cantaloupe. (If cantaloupes are not available you can eat any of the fruits given at the end of Chapter 3, where the no. 1 priority list of calorie–neutralizer fruits is given.)

Mid-morning snack: Celery stalks with cream cheese, or use Roquefort or blue cheese mixed with a low-fat yogurt. Eat two or three celery stalks; this is a fine fiber and calorie–neutralizer vegetable. You will feel satisfied until lunchtime.

Lunch: Clear consommé soup, two bowls if hungry.
Tuna fish salad with low-calorie mayonnaise.
Jello dessert with artificial whipped cream or
    stewed apricots with artificial sugar.

Dinner: Large portion of baked chicken.
Asparagus with sauce (a calorie–neutralizer
    vegetable).
Small salad, cucumbers, lettuce and tomatoes,
    with a low-calorie dressing.
Applesauce for dessert. (If homemade use
    artificial sugar, if canned, buy dietetic brand.)
Coffee, tea or skimmed milk. Use artificial sugar in
    coffee or tea.

SECOND DAY

Breakfast: All-wheat cereal (hot or cold) with skimmed milk.
A serving of strawberries or other fruit from the
    low-calorie list.
Coffee, tea or skimmed milk.

Lunch: Chopped up fresh vegetables in sour cream.
    (These can include cucumbers, green onions,
    radishes, tomatoes, green peppers and celery
    stalks cut up.) These vegetables are all
    high-fiber, calorie–neutralizers and counteract
    the rich sour cream dressing.
A slice of Cheddar or Swiss cheese.
Two pieces of rye crisp or zwieback toast.
Diet soft drink, coffee, tea or skimmed milk.

Dinner: Raw vegetable salad with dressing. (Vegetables:
    lettuce, raw mushrooms, cucumbers, green
    peppers and tomatoes.) Use any low-calorie
    dressing. (This is made up of
    calorie–neutralizer vegetables.)
Chicken soup.

Two lamb chops or favorite steak.

Banana custard pudding. (This is now available without sugar. A serving contains about 40 calories. It also comes in butterscotch or chocolate.)

Coffee, tea or skimmed milk.

THIRD DAY

Breakfast: Eggs Benedict: Poach two eggs, serve on halves of toasted English muffins. Put a slice of Canadian bacon on each muffin, and use hollandaise sauce for dressing, with a black olive on top. (Dressing recipes are given later in a special chapter.) To offset calories in this rather calorie-rich breakfast dish, eat one half a grapefruit before meal.

Lunch: Chicken salad with mayonnaise and celery.

Cucumber and tomatoes with lemon juice dressing. (These are both calorie–neutralizers and offset the mayonnaise.)

Low-calorie cheese or fruit for dessert.

Coffee, tea, skimmed milk or your favorite soft drink.

Dinner: Bowl of vegetable soup containing calorie–neutralizer vegetables.

One glass of tomato juice. (Or, calorie–neutralizer salad of tomatoes, cucumbers and lettuce, with low-calorie dressing.)

Baked bass or other fish, broiled or baked only.

Asparagus with hollandaise sauce. (See section dealing with various types of sauce.)

Fresh fruit or diet canned peaches for dessert.

FOURTH DAY

Breakfast: Glass of cranberry juice.

Bowl of whole bran (calorie–neutralizing grain) with artificial sugar.

Two eggs scrambled with margarine or Cheddar cheese omelet.

One piece of whole-wheat toast with butter.

Half-teaspoonful of jelly.

Coffee, tea or skimmed milk. Use artificial sugar in
coffee or tea.

Lunch: Broiled veal cutlet, or hamburger patty without fat.
Carrot-raisin salad.
Pineapple or peach slices.
Coffee, tea or skimmed milk, or dietetic soft drink.

Dinner: Sweetbreads on lean piece of ham.
Two slices of whole-wheat or protein bread.
Small green salad with choice of dressing.
(Calorie–neutralizer, if you use lettuce,
cucumbers, green peppers, celery and onions.)
Lemon or orange sherbet.
Usual drinks with artificial sugar.

By the fourth day you may already have registered a weight
loss of 3 to 6 pounds and this should give your morale a big
boost. However, overconfidence can be dangerous, for it is
about the fifth day that most people have an urge to stray from
their diet and eat prohibited foods. If you do this, you will find
that in the next week or two you will not only register no weight
loss whatsoever, but you will even begin to put back the weight
you have already lost.

HOW CHARLOTTE W. BEAT THE HOLIDAY BINGES

Charlotte W. felt she would have no trouble shedding 35
pounds on the calorie–neutralizer diet because of the generous
portions of food she could eat at each meal. It just happened that
Charlotte began her diet at the worst possible time, the Christmas holiday season. After the fourth day she had lost 5 pounds.
She felt confident she could easily lose the other 30 pounds to
bring her back to her normal weight.

Then the office parties started for the holidays. Dinner
invitations from friends and relatives meant being where rich
foods and drinks were served, with carbohydrate-rich desserts
of pies, cakes, ice creams and other goodies. Charlotte reasoned,
this would be only a short time until she could get back to the
diet. But when Christmas itself arrived, she went on a completely wild binge, eating the turkey with chestnut dressing,
gravy, pumpkin pie, cranberry sauce and white potatoes, as well

as sweet potatoes. Only one vegetable was served, green peas. No calorie–neutralizer fruit was served except the pumpkin, which was ruined by the added sugar and whipped cream. The next day there were turkey leftovers, and until New Year's Eve, there was feasting, drinking and partying. This completely erased the few pounds she had lost and even added a few extra pounds from all her binges!

When Charlotte reported after the holidays to the diet workshop she looked bloated and worse than before. She had to start all over again to lose the 35 pounds as well as the 3 extra pounds she had gained.

This time Charlotte was given extra calorie–neutralizer foods to reduce her craving for the calorie-rich food she had eaten during the previous two weeks. Meat remained in her diet, but the calorie–neutralizer vegetables were increased to three with lunch and dinner. All sweets, even those made with fruits, were eliminated. This was stringent, but necessary to get her back on a normal keel once again.

It took five weeks more for Charlotte to completely lose the 38 pounds, by repeating the calorie–neutralizer menus and substituting other low-calorie foods.

FIFTH DAY

Breakfast: Half a glass of apricot or prune juice. (Or, a whole orange; eat pulp and all.)

Creamed tuna on whole-wheat toast. (Or chipped beef on toast.) Make the sauce with skimmed milk and whole-wheat flour.

Usual drink with artificial sugar.

Lunch: One cup of chicken consommé.

One portion of coleslaw.

Chicken or tuna salad, with low-calorie dressing.

Two pieces zwieback toast with margarine.

Fruit cup dessert with low-calorie fruits, such as cantaloupe, watermelon, apple, and pineapple.

Dinner: Cream of tomato soup.

Twelve large mushrooms broiled in margarine.

One baked potato with real butter. (Eat the skin: This makes it more effective as a catalyst to dissolve acid ash.)

For dessert: fresh fruit in season, such as grapes, melon, figs, or strawberries.

SIXTH DAY

Breakfast: Two boiled or scrambled eggs with sausage. (Be sure to use precooked sausage with the fat removed.)

Half or whole grapefruit. (Not juices, but real fruit, as this is a valuable calorie–neutralizer and has an alkaline reaction to fight acid ash.)

Mushroom omelet, two eggs. (Use chopped ham, green peppers and onions for a western-style omelet.)

Usual hot drink with artificial sugar, real cream.

Lunch: A 4-ounce patty of ground round beef, broiled.

Portion of summer squash or zucchini. (Both are high-fiber, calorie–neutralizers.)

Tomato and cucumber salad, low-calorie dressing.

Dish of low-calorie Jello, topped with real whipped cream. (Do not be afraid of eating real cream once in a while, for remember, your body needs some fats every day. If you eat more than you should, the calorie–neutralizers will reduce the fat intake.)

Dinner: Vegetable soup containing calorie–neutralizer vegetables.

Good-sized portion of lean leg of lamb with mint jelly.

Portion of cooked spinach or string beans.

Banana whip pudding (low-calorie type available).

Usual warm drink with artificial sugar.

SEVENTH DAY

Breakfast: One whole orange or half grapefruit. (Eat the pulp to make it effective as a high-fiber, calorie–neutralizer.)

Two boiled, scrambled, or poached eggs with two strips of bacon, cooked crisp.

Usual hot drink with artificial sugar.

Lunch: One cup onion soup.
One broiled salmon steak.
One large tomato with real mayonnaise or favorite dressing.
Fruit salad (made up of calorie–neutralizers).
Usual drinks.

Dinner: Beef broth (with noodles, if preferred).
Assorted seafoods in casserole (shrimp, lobster, crab, etc.). Serve with butter and lemon sauce. (Seafood recipes are given elsewhere.)
Salad made with green peppers, radishes, cucumbers and celery. Use a rich Roquefort dressing on the salad if you wish, as it is offset by the salad ingredients.
Dessert: fruit compote (made up of calorie–neutralizer fruits).

WHAT TO EXPECT AFTER YOUR FIRST WEEK ON THE CALORIE–NEUTRALIZER DIET

You have had one week of what amounts to gourmet eating. Yet, if you check your scales, you will find you have lost 8 to 12 pounds, depending on your metabolism. If you followed this first week's diet carefully, you will have eaten a variety of foods that were pleasing to your taste buds, and which kept you from being hungry.

Despite the fact you have had a diet that seems normal, your caloric intake has been low and the calorie–neutralizer fruits, vegetables and grains have been apportioned carefully to keep your body from absorbing the fat calories you did eat.

Don't worry if you did not lose all the weight you desired this first week. Now you can have a more relaxed attitude toward dieting. By staying on the calorie–neutralizer diet another week or two you can shed another 10 to 15 pounds easily. Keep repeating the reducing menus for as long as you wish to continue losing weight. If your problem is severe and you need to lose from 30 to 60 more pounds, you can do so pleasantly and easily by repeating each week's menus and then substituting other calorie–neutralizer foods that will be given later.

HELEN C. OVERCAME HER DISCOURAGEMENT AND LOST 45 POUNDS

Helen C. told me she could never remain on any reducing diet for more than two weeks. She said that she became terribly nervous and apprehensive and began to panic in the third week, going off the diet completely.

As Helen was 45 pounds overweight and had been for several years, I realized it would be most difficult to remove that many pounds quickly without endangering her health.

For the first two weeks Helen used the regular calorie–neutralizer diet, and ate her fill of all the fruits and vegetables on the permitted lists. She also ate plenty of between-meal snacks that were so low in calories that they were easily offset by the calorie–neutralizer foods.

Helen lost 18 pounds in those two weeks. She felt so good about dieting that she repeated the menus another two weeks, losing 20 more pounds. Then she went on the extension diet, which permitted her a wider variety of foods than before, until she lost the entire 45 pounds and was down to her normal 118 pounds. Helen looked wonderful; she had no sagging flesh from losing so much weight; her health miraculously improved, and she had more energey than ever before.

YOU ARE NOW READY TO BEGIN YOUR SECOND WEEK OF DIETING

On the second week of calorie–neutralizer menus you can expect to lose anywhere from 8 to 12 pounds.

As breakfasts are most important, you will notice in the second week's menus that you will be allowed to eat a rather big breakfast. By eating some calorie–neutralizer fruits at this meal you will also be able to reduce the calorie intake so you continue to lose weight.

You can even eat some carbohydrate cereal, if you wish, such as bran, corn products, oatmeal or cream of wheat, without being afraid those extra calories will turn into fat. You do need some carbohydrates and breakfast time is probably the best time to eat them. Some people skip breakfast altogether when dieting, thinking that by cutting down on those extra calories they will lose weight more rapidly. This is wrong. When your stomach has no food all night, it requires more food to give you the energy you will need for that day's activity. The new calorie-neutralizer diet gives you enough carbohydrates each day to make up the required amount of 50 to 60 grams a day. Carbohydrates give you energy by nourishing muscles and tissues, and keep your blood sugar level high enough to keep you from being nervous, tense, depressed or suffering from dizziness, weakness and extreme fatigue. This is especially important while you are losing weight, for when the extra pounds begin to melt away, you will have no fat deposits to draw on in reserve, to keep you from suffering symptoms that come from malnutrition.

MYRTLE C. SKIPPED BREAKFAST
TO LOSE WEIGHT FASTER

Myrtle C. had never been one who craved big breakfasts. "So early in the morning I am repelled by food," she told me, "so I have always skipped breakfast. Outside of a cup of coffee, I seldom eat solid food until lunch." But despite this fact, Myrtle admitted she had somehow gained 35 pounds in the past two years.

Myrtle began the usual calorie–neutralizer menus but made one important change: She still did not eat the breakfasts that were on the menu. She had only one cup of black coffee, with no cream or sweetener. That first week she lost 10 pounds, and proclaimed triumphantly at our next meeting, "You see, I don't need breakfasts to lose weight. Your calorie–neutralizer diet is working!"

On the second week Myrtle had another story to report. She skipped breakfast again, but by noon she was so hungry that she ate more food than the reducing menu called for, indulging her sweet tooth. She added ice cream to her meal; on another day she added an extra hamburger with a roll; on the third day, during her coffee break, she ate two doughnuts and a cup of coffee. If Myrtle had followed these forbidden foods with sufficient calorie–neutralizer vegetables, fruits and low-calorie foods, she could have handled the extra calories and they would have been neutralized. But she didn't. After the second week she found that she had lost only 3 pounds. Once again she became discouraged, insisting that no diet system ever worked for her.

By skipping breakfasts, Myrtle had lowered her blood sugar to such an extent that her body called for more foods at lunch and dinner to make up for her dietary deficiency. This was what was keeping her weight on. I told her that her weight would *increase* if she persisted in her habit of skipping breakfasts and then indulging her appetite the rest of the day.

Myrtle started the very next day to have a hearty breakfast. She had between-meals snacks of fruits and vegetables in the no. 1 calorie–neutralizer category, with a good lunch and dinner, and even bedtime snacks, of the low-calorie foods. The next week Myrtle was delighted to find she had shed 10 pounds. The next week she took off another 12 pounds. It was no effort to stay on the diet once she learned the importance of having a good breakfast. Myrtle then went on the sustaining diet given in Chapter 12 and had no further weight problems.

If you are inclined to skip breakfast or any meal, with the excuse that you are not hungry, remember that your body will suffer the consequences. You will reduce your blood sugar levels and your hunger-stat will blast away demanding carbohydrate foods like ice cream, cake, pie, doughnuts and spaghetti. Because you are so hungry, it will seem natural for you to eat these calorie-rich foods to satisfy your craving for immediate nourishment.

EXPECT TO LOSE 8 TO 12 POUNDS THIS SECOND WEEK OF THE CALORIE–NEUTRALIZER DIET

Depending on your particular metabolism, you can expect to lose from 8 to 12 pounds more on the new calorie–neutralizer diet this second week. You can substitute meats and fishes to please your appetite, as long as you adhere to the general diet and eat sufficient amounts of calorie–neutralizer foods with each meal. You will be allowed generous portions of foods in such a wide variety that you will not be bored one single day.

SECOND WEEK MENUS

FIRST DAY

Breakfast: One whole grapefruit, or two whole oranges. Eat the pulp of the fruit, not just the juice, as this is a high calorie–neutralizer fruit.
Sausage soufflé, scrambled eggs with a little milk.
One slice of whole-wheat toast.
Coffee, tea or skimmed milk. Use real cream in coffee and artificial sugar.

Lunch: Cheeseburger with two slices of bacon on roll.
Small salad of cucumbers, tomatoes and green peppers, with low-calorie dressing. This furnishes a good portion of calorie–neutralizers to take care of any extra calories in the cheeseburger and bacon.
Gelatin or custard pudding.
Dietetic soft drink or coffee, tea or skimmed milk.

Dinner: Pot roast.
Boiled, new potatoes.
Celery stalks, radishes, cucumber slices, tomatoes. These vegetables eaten before the meal will furnish fiber bulk and calorie–neutralizers.
Lemon custard dessert (quick-setting, low-calorie brands are now on the market).

SECOND DAY

Breakfast: Two soft-boiled eggs. Crumble two slices of crisp bacon and eat with one piece of whole-wheat toast.
Whole bran cereal with real cream, artificial sugar. This furnishes sufficient calorie–neutralizer and fiber to keep calories from being turned into fat.
Coffee, tea or milk.

Lunch: Tuna fish or salmon salad on roll, with melted
               cheese on top.
               Crisp lettuce and cucumber salad with low-calorie
               dressing.
               Butterscotch pudding (low-calorie).
               Usual drink.

Dinner: Green pea soup.
               Antipasto of salami, ham, green peppers,
               anchovies, served with herbs sprinkled on them
               and a touch of vinegar.
               Generous portion of beef liver steak. (Calf's liver
               is more expensive and not any more
               nourishing than beef.)
               Asparagus with cream sauce.
               Coffee, tea or skimmed milk.

THIRD DAY

Breakfast: Canadian bacon with two poached eggs.
               One whole-wheat English muffin, with butter and
               jam.
               Half a cantaloupe, or other in-season fruit.
               Coffee, tea or skimmed milk.

Lunch: Chicken salad with real mayonnaise, boiled eggs
               and cut-up celery stalks.
               One whole tomato.
               Piece of zwieback toast.
               Dish of sherbet or Jello.

Dinner: Tossed salad consisting of lettuce, tomatoes,
               cucumbers, onions, green peppers.
               Mixed grill with garlic butter sauce. Grill may
               consist of sausage, liver, beef or pork.
               Gelatin parfait with whipped cream. (Cream can
               be artificial variety without butterfat.)

FOURTH DAY

Breakfast: Half grapefruit or cantaloupe, if in season.
               Two fried eggs with sausage. (Use the type that
               has the fat fried out, requiring only warming in
               pan.)

Slice of whole-wheat toast, butter, marmalade.
Coffee, tea or milk.
(The grapefruit and whole-wheat toast furnish
fiber and calorie–neutralizers to take care of the
extra calories.)

Lunch: Asparagus soup.
Three meatballs with chopped onions.
Orange sherbet.
Usual tea, coffee or soft drink.

Dinner: Potted chicken made with calorie–neutralizer
vegetables, celery, onions, carrots and green
peppers.
Beet salad, serve with chopped onions, lemon
juice, one sliced cucumber and yogurt, mixed
together.
Dessert of fruit compote, either fresh or canned. (If
canned be sure it is dietetic brand without
sugar.)
Usual drink.

FIFTH DAY

Breakfast: Shirred eggs with chopped-up chicken livers.
(Mushrooms, onions or bacon chips may be
used instead.)
Applesauce (with artificial sugar).
Usual drink.

Lunch: Bowl of plain consommé.
Dish of coleslaw with onions and chopped-up
carrots.
Salmon or tuna fish salad with low-calorie
dressing.
Piece of whole-wheat toast with butter.
Gelatin for dessert.
Usual drink.

Dinner: Filet mignon broiled, with four good-sized
mushrooms.
Lettuce, cucumber and watercress salad, with
low-calorie dressing.
Several stalks of asparagus with butter sauce.

Fruit compote for dessert.
Usual drink.

SIXTH DAY

Breakfast: Honeydew melon, as much as you wish.
All-wheat cold or hot cereal with real milk or cream.
Three slices of bacon and two poached eggs.
Usual drink.

Lunch: Bowl of consommé.
Celery stalks, radishes and cucumbers.
Broiled liver.
Dessert of fresh fruit in season with cheese.
Usual drink.

Dinner: Two lamb chops broiled, or leg of lamb with mint
jelly.
Diced, cooked carrots.
Green peas.
Cold zucchini salad. (Boil and let cool, slice and
serve with a touch of vinegar and garlic oil.)
Canned peaches or pineapple (dietetic type).
Usual drink.

SEVENTH DAY

Breakfast: Sweetbreads on whole-wheat toast.
Half a grapefruit with artificial sweetener.
Whole-wheat cereal.
Coffee, tea or skimmed milk.

Lunch: Ground round patty, broiled.
Baked potato or potatoes rissole.
Fruit salad made of fresh or canned fruits, such as
pineapple, peaches, apricots and cherries. The
calorie–neutralizer fruits take care of the
calories in the potato with real butter for flavor.
Cheese slice for dessert.
Usual drink.

Dinner: Baked or broiled fish with lemon sauce.
Green salad with low-calorie dressing.
Custard pudding (low-calorie prepared type).
Usual drink.

These two weeks of the calorie–neutralizer reducing diet can be repeated for another two weeks if you find that you need to lose more than 20 pounds. A later chapter tells further how to. extend this diet if you need to lose 30 to 60 extra pounds.

SOME POINTS TO OBSERVE
DURING THIS TWO-WEEK PERIOD

1. Don't let yourself become so hungry that you are tempted to go back to your former eating habits. Between meal snacks are permitted during this two-week period. You can have soup or leftover meat from dinner, or munch on celery, radishes, cucumbers and green peppers until your appetite is satisfied. You can also have a whole cantaloupe, honeydew melon or watermelon when in season.

2. Try to avoid salt as much as possible. The body needs sodium, but table salt is sodium chloride, which is labeled "poison" when sold in drug stores. Your body can get all the sodium it needs from the calorie–neutralizer vegetables. Extra table salt during your dieting may add up to 10 or 15 pounds of false weight by storing water in your body cells.

3. If you need to lose more than 15 or 20 pounds and have to go on a prolonged diet for one to two months, it is best to check periodically with your physician to be sure you remain in good condition. Although there is nothing in the new calorie–neutralizer diet that would be harmful to the average person, those suffering from any form of disorder, such as diabetes or hypoglycemia, should be sure they can continue a prolonged diet without harm.

4. Refrain from eating white sugar, honey or other sweeteners during this two-week period, as they are high forms of carbohydrates. You will be eating as many as 45 to 60 grams of carbohydrates in the natural calorie–neutralizer vegetables and fruits, so you will not suffer from low energy.

5. Although in these two weeks of calorie–neutralizer reducing menus you are given meat as often as twice a day, you may feel better eating meat only once a day. If so, you may eat two or more of the calorie–neutralizer vegetables and fruits on

the list for lunch, and save the main meat meal for dinner. Overeating meat—even though it is protein—can add calories to a meal, so it should be restricted to a small serving of about 4 ounces at a meal. Also, when you use the calorie–neutralizer vegetables and fruits with the meat meal, you keep the body from absorbing all those rich calories.

6. Should you drink fruit juices during this two-week period of dieting? No. Fruit juices are high in quickly-absorbed sugars and carbohydrates, making it simple for the digestive tract to assimilate them as fat calories. It is better to eat a whole orange or grapefruit, for the fiber content of the pulp helps delay the digestive processes. You can eat an apple, orange, strawberries or blueberries with milk and artificial sugar as between-meal snacks, and they will not be absorbed as quickly by the body or turned into fat cells.

7. After a full dinner, avoid eating again before retiring at night. Your body does not need those extra calories while you sleep and they will turn into fat very quickly.

CHAPTER 5

Calorie–Neutralizer Buffer Foods That Give Variety to Your Diet

In any prolonged period of dieting it is important to add what I call "buffer foods." These keep your diet from becoming monotonous and at the same time furnish your body with adequate amounts of tasty, nutritious foods.

This chapter gives a wide variety of calorie–neutralizer foods that you can intersperse with the reducing menus in Chapter 4, and many other foods that you may substitute for some of those given in the daily reducing menus.

RICH PROTEIN MEALS ARE POSSIBLE ON THE CALORIE–NEUTRALIZER DIET

You have already seen that you are permitted to have rich protein meals while losing as many pounds as you choose. For instance, for some breakfasts you can have two eggs with three strips of bacon. Be sure you have a calorie–neutralizer fruit, such as half a cantaloupe or grapefruit, before breakfast. You can have chipped, creamed beef on a slice of whole-wheat toast. Try scrambled eggs with calf's brains; it's considered a delicacy by many gourmets. A two-egg omelet can be served with any of the following ingredients: mushrooms, diced ham, green peppers and onions, Cheddar cheese, cream cheese or jelly.

A 5-ounce patty cheeseburger, for lunch, can be easily offset, even if eaten on a bun, by having a calorie–neutralizer salad of lettuce, cucumbers, green peppers and tomatoes with a low-calorie dressing. A full variation dinner is possible by having two lamb chops broiled, with any vegetable you choose, or six shrimps, with a dressing of mayonnaise mixed with ketchup, preceded by a big calorie–neutralizer green salad. For dessert, eat any portion of calorie–neutralizer fruits. You can even add rich desserts, which I shall give in a later chapter, by utilizing those fruits that are in the calorie–neutralizer list.

HOW BUFFER FOODS HELPED
ROBERT D. LOSE 50 POUNDS

Robert D. was a truck driver and he had been in the habit of eating at truck stops. Most of his meals were of the meat, potatoes and pie variety. Occasionally he would stop for coffee with cream and sugar, and some doughnuts, cake, pie or ice cream. He also carried sandwiches of white bread with various types of meat, peanut butter, or sliced turkey or chicken, heavy with butter and mayonnaise. No wonder that, at 5 feet 10 inches, he soon tipped the scales at 215 pounds.

When Robert began the calorie–neutralizer diet to lose 50 pounds he feared that he would not be able to keep from being hungry. He had tried three other diets to lose weight and had given up each time after a week or two because he felt constantly hungry on the limited calories he was allowed.

Robert began the calorie–neutralizer diet by having a hearty breakfast of two poached eggs with three strips of bacon, two cups of coffee with real cream and artificial sugar.

He carried in his lunch box sandwiches made without bread. Slices of bologna were rolled around creamed cheese or

Cheddar cheese. He also carried calorie–neutralizer vegetables to eat with lunch or as snacks, consisting of celery stalks, cucumbers, tomatoes, radishes, green peppers and lettuce. Because he had such a hearty appetite, Robert ate big dinners at home, using a wide variety of meats given in the list of protein meats that follow: steak, liver, roast lamb, sweetbreads or ground chuck. He always ate the meat with two or three of the calorie–neutralizer vegetables, such as asparagus, cabbage, spinach, broccoli or cauliflower au gratin. Fruits furnished him with desserts, especially melons, strawberries, apples and cherries. He carried oranges in his lunch box and ate as many as three a day.

The first week Robert registered only 8 pounds loss, but the second and third weeks he lost 12 pounds and 13 pounds. The other 17 pounds were lost in two more weeks. At the end of his diet Robert tipped the scales at 165 pounds, an ideal weight for his age and height.

If your appetite is increased by heavy work or other unusual circumstances, the extra buffer foods, when added to the regular calorie–neutralizer diet, can help you continue losing weight without suffering from hunger or feeling frustrated because of the small amount of food eaten.

CHOOSE FROM A VARIETY OF GOOD DINNER FOODS

Here are some other dinner choices that will satisfy your hunger-stat and will assure you of receiving a well-balanced, nutritious meal, utilizing the three elements any normal diet should contain: carbohydrates, proteins and fats.

For dinner, try four slices of bacon (fat cooked out) with two eggs cooked in any style. Or, have two slices of roast beef, followed by half a grapefruit, strawberries, blueberries, melon or any other fruit on the calorie–neutralizer list.

Treat yourself to some coffee with real cream for dinner. Heavy table cream is actually less fattening than milk, for it contains less carbohydrates than milk's 12 grams per cupful. There is a very small amount of carbohydrate in heavy cream if you use only about one tablespoonful in your coffee, and it does give a rich feeling to end your meal with a good cup of coffee.

Still another filling protein dinner could consist of two broiled frankfurters, or three hamburgers, or half a dozen shrimps, or a two-egg omelet. Another suggestion: try a big shrimp cocktail, half a pound of broiled liver with onions, and two of the vegetables given in the calorie–neutralizer priority list.

In all of these variation diets you can include all lean meats and fish, but not pork, as it is too rich in calories. The meats and fish should be broiled, and all the fat cut off.

In place of the meats given in the regular calorie–neutralizer reducing menus you can substitute a 4-ounce portion of ground round steak, a piece of veal or roast beef, a small broiled steak or any of the following low-calorie fishes:

sea bass	fresh tuna
cod steaks	abalone
flounder	shrimp
raw oysters	shad roe
salmon (boiled or broiled)	

To this wide variety of fish products you may add any of the following low-calorie meats:

ground chuck	sirloin steak, broiled
(with all fat removed)	sweetbreads
filet mignon	T-bone steak
kidneys	tripe
heart	lamb (lean)
liver	lamb chops
ground round	leg of veal or veal cutlets
pot roast	(with fat removed)

You must not eat excessive amounts of even these meats however, for remember, more than 4 ounces at one meal can add extra calories. Since you are allowed to eat such a wide variety of rich foods, you can easily limit the amount of meat you eat until you have lost the required weight.

While you are on this variation diet you can also add some low-calorie dairy products as buffer foods. These will keep you from being hungry but do not add extra rich calories. You will still continue to lose weight using these dairy products, but not as rapidly as you did on the strict calorie–neutralizer diet.

    cottage cheese
    skimmed milk
    buttermilk
    yogurt (without added fruit and sugar)

You may also have poached or boiled eggs whenever you feel hungry between meals or for breakfast, when on this variation diet.

If you find that you are constantly hungry between meals and you must have snacks, stick to the low-calorie foods and don't go off on a carbohydrate kick that will immediately put on fat. The following case from my files shows the dangers of such a practice.

DAN B. WENT FROM 160 TO 240 POUNDS IN THREE YEARS

When Dan B. began tipping the scales at 240 pounds, he was not alarmed. He was nearly six feet tall, had a big-boned frame, and figured his hours at the gym each weekend would take care of his weight problem.

However, Dan soon found that no matter how many barbells he lifted, and no matter how often he jogged or played handball, the pounds simply did not melt away. In fact, his appetite grew by leaps and bounds. The more exercise he did, the more calories his body demanded and they were usually of the fattening kind.

His wife Betty, who was herself 25 pounds overweight, finally brought Dan to our workshop for help.

In taking their case histories, for they both wanted to lose weight, I found that Betty was really the guilty one who had gotten her husband off to the wrong dietary start after their marriage three years ago.

Dan was a punch-press operator in a factory that made steel parts for various products. He sat all day and fed strips of steel into his punch press, expending very little physical energy. His wife wanted to be sure he had a good lunch so she usually packed two or three sandwiches. These consisted of ham and cheese, with mayonnaise and mustard, peanut butter and jelly, and often tuna fish made with mayonnaise and onions, and always on white bread.

During his coffee break, as well as at lunch time, Dan sought out the nearby diner, where he ate pie, cake, ice cream, and sometimes puddings or jello. He frequently stopped at the diner twice a day, having two cups of coffee with sugar and cream, as well as some dessert.

Dinners for Dan and Betty were carbohydrate contests to see who could consume the greatest number of calorie-rich foods. Because she did not go to work, Betty had all day to plan her deadly bill of fare for each dinner. She specialized in Italian cooking, with lots of olive oil, garlic, tomato paste and onions. She was expert at baking pies, seven-layer cakes, and cookies that promised heavenly enjoyment and pounds and pounds of fat to those who had the courage to consume them.

Dan began putting on weight during their honeymoon to Niagara Falls. They rented a cabin where they had their own kitchen and Betty practiced her cuisine on her adoring participant. They both put on several pounds and laughed off the evidence of the scales after returning to their more prosaic daily routine.

As the months passed and each gained more unsightly pounds it was no longer a laughing matter. Dan and Betty knew something was wrong with their food plan and that they must seek help before they developed illnesses from being overweight.

I made out a diet schedule that excluded most of the calorie-rich carbohydrates they both loved, and gave them lists of all the calorie–neutralizer fruits and vegetables they could substitute, so they could both eat all they wanted without fearing they would add extra pounds.

It took Dan a little more than eight weeks to lose 80 pounds on the calorie–neutralizer diet, for there was a need to wean him from his carbohydrate hunger. He still carried his lunch box, but now the sandwiches were bologna wrapped around cheese, and celery stalks, radishes, cucumbers and sliced tomatoes, to eat whenever he was hungry. He also carried fresh fruits with him and ate plenty of cantaloupe and watermelon when he got hungry at home while watching TV.

Meat and two calorie–neutralizer vegetables for dinner, with a big green salad, and sometimes soup before dinner, curbed Dan and Betty's appetite until bedtime, when they both usually had snacks of more fruits or vegetables. In this way they never really got too hungry and soon were able to get rid of their craving for carbohydrates and sweets.

Betty lost her 25 pounds in three weeks time. From then on she stayed on the sustaining diet, being sure that Dan kept to the calorie–neutralizer food plan until he had shed his excess 80 pounds. Then they both went on the sustaining diet that gave them a balanced, nutritional food plan for life, and each admitted to feeling better than when they carried all those excess pounds.

WIDE VARIETY OF
CALORIE–NEUTRALIZER FRUITS CAN BE USED

You can choose from a wide variety of calorie–neutralizer fruits while you are on this reducing diet. These can be eaten raw, stewed or in salads. You can fill up on any of these high priority calorie–neutralizer fruits without ever fearing that they will put on an ounce of fat. In fact, they will act as catalysts to drive out acid ash and to reduce caloric intake, because the fruits given in this diet take more calories to digest than they give to your body! This alone makes them valuable aids in reducing. Eat these fruits before heavy meals, or as desserts: cantaloupe, honeydew melon, watermelon, strawberries, cherries, pumpkin, or rhubarb.

What about drinking orange juice or other fruit juices? Juices are fine in your future extension diet, when you have lost the desired weight, but while you are on the reducing diet you should avoid fruit or vegetable juices for this reason: Liquids furnish no resistance to the digestive tract and are almost immediately assimilated in the metabolic process. Many of these

juices are rich in carbohydrates, which means they turn into fat
quickly.

FRUIT AND VEGETABLE JUICES INCREASED HER WEIGHT

Ruth T. tried several different diets to lose her ungainly 30
excess pounds, and each time she failed. She came into the
diet workshop complaining that she doubted if even the calorie–neutralizer diet would help her. She had previously tried
diets that emphasized plenty of proteins, with low carbohydrates, and some vegetables and fruits, but Ruth had added to
her menus three or four glasses of orange juice, carrot juice and
other vegetable juices each day. When I pointed out that these
various fruits and vegetable juices were quickly absorbed by the
digestive tract without having to be digested, she understood
why she had been unable to lose weight. The juices were alkaline in their effect, but as liquids, they required no great effort
to digest, so they were quickly absorbed into the body and
turned into fat. All the dieting in the world cannot overcome this
form of carbohydrate absorption.

Ruth began to eat the whole orange or grapefruit for breakfast, and not the juice. By cutting out the vegetable juices, she
began to have immediate results. She easily lost her 30 pounds
in a little over three weeks of dieting.

EAT THE WHOLE FRUIT FOR CALORIE–NEUTRALIZER EFFECT

By eating the whole fruit, pulp and all, the fruit is digested
more slowly, using up more calories. Such fruits as apples,
oranges, grapefruit, pineapples, apricots, peaches and melons
are all calorie–neutralizers. Also, as such fruits are alkaline in
their chemical reaction, they immediately begin to work on the
acid ash to help flush it out of the body before it has a chance to
accumulate in the cells as fatty tissue.

Orange juice contains 3 grams of carbohydrates per ounce.
A 10-ounce glass each morning immediately gives you as much
as 30 grams of fattening carbohydrates. While dieting it is wise to

keep the carbohydrate intake down to about 45 grams a day. If you worry that you do not get enough vitamin C each day, you can eat cantaloupes in season, or a whole grapefruit a day, or you can use green peppers, carrots and celery in preparing your daily reducing menus. Start your day by taking the juice of a lemon in a glass of water half an hour before breakfast. This will give you a sufficient amount of vitamin C to last all day.

EXTEND THE LIST OF
CALORIE–NEUTRALIZER FRUITS AFTER TWO WEEKS

When you have been on the calorie–neutralizer diet for two weeks and have lost from 10 to 20 pounds, and you need to lose more weight, you can do this more slowly by adding the following fruits to your daily diet. Some, like apples, cantaloupe and watermelon, were in priority list no. 1. The others can now be added safely. You will still lose weight but it will be for a more extended period of time.

apples	cantaloupe	lemons
apricots	strawberries	tangerines
cherries	pears	pineapple
oranges	peaches	papaya
watermelon	grapes	bananas

Most fruits should be eaten raw, but if you cannot obtain fresh fruits then you can use the canned dietetic, sugar-free fruits that are available in most markets.

MOST CALORIE–NEUTRALIZERS HIGH IN FIBER BULK

Most of the calorie–neutralizer vegetables and fruits given in this new reducing diet are valuable because they furnish the body with bulk and fiber. When this enters the digestive system it slows down the process of metabolization and neutralizes calorie absorption. Foods leave the body quicker, preventing conversion into fat cells. Also, as these calorie–neutralizer fruits and vegetables are alkaline in their chemical reaction, they tend to dissolve and flush out the harmful acid ash that gathers in the body.

WATER CONSUMPTION IMPORTANT
IN FLUSHING OUT HARMFUL ACID ASH

To help flush out acid ash and make it easier to dissolve fat cells while dieting, drink at least eight glasses of water a day. Acid ash is also released through the skin when you perspire, and this extra water is needed by your body to help in this process. If the acid ash is not released, it can cause fat deposits in your skin. Take a hot bath each day and rub the body with a rough towel to dry; this can help the skin get rid of acid ash deposits.

While you are dieting, avoid drinking iced water or soft drinks. This can be a shock to your entire system. Drink when thirsty, keep the water cold but without ice, and avoid all soft drinks while dieting, unless they are the dietetic kind. It is wise to drink a full glass of water upon retiring, as this helps flush out the kidneys and avoids the formation of kidney stones. The average person drinks too little water, so the body fats and acid ash cannot be properly eliminated.

CALORIES DO COUNT
WHEN YOU GO OVER 3000
FOR THE DAY

Although the new calorie–neutralizer diet helps tremendously in neutralizing calories when eaten in excess, there is still a limit to the number of calories you can consume while losing weight. When you go over 3000 calories a day, your problem will be greater because this is way beyond the allotted number allowed while on a diet. The following example reveals clearly what happens in such cases.

COMPUTER OPERATOR CONSUMED
3000 CALORIES A DAY AND GAINED 35 POUNDS

Susan L., 24, was a computer operator who normally weighed 128 pounds. Her work was of a sedentary nature, so when her weight began going up until it was 153 pounds, she knew something had to be done immediately.

When Susan came into the diet workshop, I found she was consuming 3000 or more calories a day on a rich diet that was more suitable to a truck driver than to a computer operator who did not do much physical work.

Susan ate little breakfast, mostly coffee and doughnuts, or two pieces of white toast with butter and marmalade. She felt by skimping on breakfast she could eat more at lunch and dinner. But by mid-morning her blood-sugar level was so low that her hunger-stat screamed for something to eat, and that meant carbohydrates. Susan then ate two candy bars, a dish of ice cream, or a piece of pie. She would drink a glass of milk or a cup of coffee with two spoonfuls of sugar and cream. By lunch she still craved carbohydrates, so it was a big burger, French fries and milkshake. By late afternoon she would again have a candy bar or sugar-filled soft drink—or both.

At dinner Susan ate a truck driver's meal of meat, creamed vegetables, gravy on potatoes, white bread, butter, more coffee and cream and sugar, and a rich dessert of pie, cake or ice cream.

In Susan's case calories did count, and it didn't take a computer to reckon how high that count went. She was consuming more calories than any woman her age, height and caloric-expenditure required. Susan really should have been eating about 2000 calories, and when she began the calorie–neutralizer diet to lose her 37 pounds, I cut her down even less to 1500 calories a day.

Susan ate a heavier breakfast than normal, so she would not suffer hunger pangs in mid-morning. She was allowed between-meal snacks, but they were all in the calorie–neutralizer class of vegetables and fruits. Her lunch still had to be hearty, so she would not suffer blood-sugar depletion before dinner. She still ate the hambuger, but without bread, and she still had her dessert, but it was made up of fruits, puddings (low-calorie) and such foods as applesauce, stewed fruits and jello.

At dinner Susan ate a good portion of meat, fish or chicken, with two calorie–neutralizer vegetables from the no. 1 priority list, and always a big salad with low-calorie dressing.

On this diet Susan began to lose from 8 to 12 pounds a week, and never once reverted to her old high-calorie habits. In exactly four weeks, she was once again 128 pounds. She then went on the lifetime sustaining diet and knew she would never again have a weight problem.

BETWEEN-MEAL SNACKS SHOULD BE
ONLY CALORIE–NEUTRALIZER FOODS

Many times a person on the calorie–neutralizer diet feels that he or she can snack between meals and still lose weight. Remember, the calorie–neutralizer foods you eat during your regular meals keep your body from absorbing the fat calories you ingest. However, the wrong kind of between-meal snacks do not have the benefit of such neutralizing foods. If they are in the fat and carbohydrate category, they will quickly be turned into fat by your metabolism.

To avoid this, keep a constant supply of calorie–neutralizer foods in your refrigerator. When you are hungry you can nibble on these.

Some of these calorie–neutralizer snacks are:

sliced cucumbers
celery stalks (filled with low-calorie cheeses)
tomato slices
green peppers
raw carrots
radishes

You can also eat any of the calorie–neutralizer fruits given in the priority list no. 1 between meals. Such fruits as cantaloupe, watermelon, strawberries, apples, oranges and grapefruit will not add extra fat calories but will satisfy your appetite and furnish bulk for the digestive track. Also the natural sugars they give you will increase your blood-sugar levels and give you greater energy and endurance.

CHAPTER 6

The Calorie–Neutralizer Foods That Supply Valuable Vitamins While Reducing

Many nutritionists and medical experts warn of the dangers that dieters encounter while trying to lose weight. Most of the foods that must be eliminated while dieting contain many essential nutritional elements such as vitamins, minerals, fats and carbohydrates, which are important in maintaining the body in good health.

In the new calorie–neutralizer diet to lose weight, you will receive all the vitamins and minerals your body requires and never suffer from the nutritional imbalance that impairs many reducing diets. This is especially true if you are trying to lose only 15 to 20 pounds. Even if you go on the calorie–neutralizer diet for two or three months to lose an additional 50 to 100 pounds, you can include certain calorie–neutralizer foods and obtain all the vitamins, minerals and other elements your body needs.

AMERICANS: THE BEST-FED PEOPLE
AND THE POOREST NOURISHED

Scientists and nutritionists estimate that Americans are among the best-fed people in the world but the poorest nourished. Most diets are deficient in some of the most important elements of nutrition. Obviously, this condition becomes exaggerated when dieting to lose weight. On such a stringent diet most fattening foods are completely eliminated and there is danger of depriving the body of some essential nutrients and vitamins.

Scientists who have done research on the dietary deficiencies suffered by 50 million Americans have found that even when not dieting to lose weight, Americans suffer from a wide variety of such disorders as digestive disturbances, bad teeth, fatigue, nervousness, constipation, skin trouble, arthritis, high blood pressure and heart trouble. Many of these ailments might be avoided by a balanced diet that includes foods which contain all the essential vitamins, minerals and other elements the body needs for good health.

THE BUILT-IN SAFETY FEATURES
OF THE NEW CALORIE–NEUTRALIZER DIET

I have carefully researched the chemistry of various food combinations to find out how to limit the fattening foods and increase the low-calorie foods in the new calorie–neutralizer diet. I retained those foods, even when they were carbohydrates or fats, that would assure you of a balanced diet in which all the required vitamins and minerals will be present. Then I carefully apportioned for each day's menus sufficient calorie–neutralizer foods such as vegetables, grains, and fruits, so that even when you occasionally eat foods high in calories the fat will be eliminated in the form of acid ash. These high-fiber, alkaline foods cannot make you fat, and it is safe to eat them in larger quantities than you could in most reducing diets.

You can select the various foods in the calorie–neutralizer lists that you enjoy, and include them in your daily menus, thus assuring you that you will be getting the necessary vitamins the body needs each day.

How to Obtain Vitamin A

Vitamin A can be obtained in natural foods, many of which are calorie–neutralizers. This important vitamin helps protect you against infections. It is vital to human fertilization and the growth of the embryo. There are often childbirth disturbances when Vitamin A is lacking in the mother's diet. It is also thought to be important in the bone formation of the growing child. Lack of Vitamin A is also thought to affect digestion adversely and to cause respiratory disturbances. Scientists now believe that this vitamin helps slow down the age process and promote a longer life.

Foods That Contain Vitamin A

This vitamin can be found in many of the vegetables and fruits included in the calorie–neutralizer reducing menus. Many high-fiber green vegetables are rich in vitamin A, including squash, turnip greens, broccoli, dandelions, collards and mustard greens.

You can also receive vitamin A in yellow fruits and vegetables, such as apricots, cantaloupes and yellow squash. Carrots are another popular source.

A rich source of vitamin A is found in fish liver oils, liver, eggs, cream and butter. A little cream and butter in the calorie–neutralizer diet will not add fat to the body but will assure you of having sufficient vitamin A each day of your diet. It has now been found that the body puts on fat more rapidly when it is deprived of vitamin A.

DIANA R. HAD TWO MISCARRIAGES DUE TO LACK OF VITAMIN A

The full impact of what can happen to people, especially women, who are denied certain vitamins, came to my attention when Diana R. told me her story. She had been 25 pounds overweight when she became pregnant. Diana went on a diet to lose weight, reducing her food intake to fewer than 1000 calories and cutting out most of the foods which contain vitamin A, such as green vegetables and yellow fruits. She ate only meat and salads and cottage cheese, with some milk products. Diana lost weight, despite the fact she was pregnant and needed more food to feed the growing child within her womb. Within three months after pregnancy, she had a miscarriage and was seriously ill from loss of blood.

She became pregnant again after gaining the weight back that she had formerly lost. She resumed her diet and the same thing happened. Diana began to fear she could never have a child. Doctors told her this was the case with many women, so she tried to forget about children. When she began to rapidly gain weight once more until she was 50 pounds overweight, she came to the weight control workshop and learned about the value of vitamins, even while dieting. This time she began to lose weight safely and normally. When she had lost 25 pounds she found she was once again pregnant. Now in her diet she included plenty of vitamin A by eating yellow fruits, apricots, cantaloupes, as well as leafy green vegetables, yellow squash, mustard greens and other vegetables heavy in vitamin A. At the end of the nine-month period, she gave birth to a normal, healthy 8-pound baby girl.

It is not only women who need this important vitamin; men also can benefit from taking vitamin A. It can so easily be obtained from natural foods that no one should suffer negative results from its absence in the diet while reducing.

Vitamin B-1

Vitamin B-1 is essential to the metabolization of carbohydrates. This vitamin is called thiamine. It helps break down the sugars in the diet that give the body energy.

Insufficient amounts of B-1 in your diet can cause fatigue, nausea, psychic and emotional disturbances, poor appetite, leg cramps and sensations of numbness in various parts of the body, such as the fingers, legs and toes. Lack of this important vitamin can also lead to periods of deep moodiness and depression.

Nutritionists call vitamin B-1 the vitality vitamin. It can be obtained in many of the calorie–neutralizer foods such as brown rice, soybeans, brewer's yeast, wheat germ, beef kidneys, beef heart, oysters, some pork products and eggs. Avoid over-cooking these foods, as excessive heat is known to destroy this vitamin.

The important B complex vitamins also include riboflavin (B-2) niacin (B-6) and pyridoxine (B-12). A brief explanation of each vitamin in the B family follows that tells you what they do for the body and lists the calorie–neutralizer foods that contain them.

Vitamin B-2 (Riboflavin)

A lack of this important vitamin can lead to distressing eye conditions, such as itching, burning and a bloodshot appearance.

B-2 also helps the body retain its youthful resiliency and seems to retard the aging process. It is also helpful in avoiding skin disorders such as dandruff and eczema. Loss of hair is attributed to a lack of this vitamin. It can also lead to mental depression and a generally diminished vitality that affects sexual potency.

Vitamin B-2 can be found in the following calorie–neutralizer foods: eggs, milk, cheese, wheat germ, brewer's yeast, liver, green vegetables, peas, lima beans, yogurt, whole-wheat cereals and flour. Plenty of yeast and liver will assure you of obtaining sufficient riboflavin in your diet.

Vitamin B-6 (Pyridoxine)

This vitamin is important in human nutrition, for it assists in the metabolizing of proteins and helps form antibodies that fight germ infections and assist in healing. It is also known to have a sedative effect on the nerves and improves muscle tone.

Physicians are studying the effects of using vitamin B-6 in the treatment of muscular dystrophy and multiple sclerosis, as well as in the treatment of other disorders affecting the nerves and muscles.

Most of the calorie–neutralizer foods contain this important vitamin, including whole-wheat foods, bran and cereals, as well as most meats. The fiber-rich calorie–neutralizer fresh, green vegetables like spinach, broccoli, asparagus, watercress, beet tops, turnip greens and other leafy green vegetables are rich in vitamin B-6. Liver is also a good source of this vitamin. Most of the calorie–neutralizer menus for reducing contain foods that are rich in vitamin B-6.

LACK OF VITAMIN B-6 LED TO
SEVERE SKIN DISTURBANCES

Wanda C. was only 15 pounds overweight when she sought out my guidance. She had suffered for one year with unsightly eczema and skin rash on her face and arms. She couldn't wear make-up because it aggravated her condition. Because of these afflictions she was highly nervous and depressed. Her husband had left her six months before, and she had seriously considered committing suicide because of her severe depression.

Wanda had checked with her doctor several times as to the reason for her skin condition. He had prescribed various ointments, which she used, but they had no effect. She felt it might be something connected with her weight problem so she joined the diet workshop to see if that would help her.

Wanda began a special calorie–neutralizer diet that fit her exact needs. She included lean meats in the daily menus, liver once a week, and each day she ate at least two of the leafy green vegetables that contained vitamin B-6. She also had whole-wheat cereals and oatmeal for breakfast, and added one cube of yeast a day to her food intake.

Wanda lost the extra 15 pounds easily within two weeks. More important to Wanda was that the extra vitamin B-6 she received in her calorie–neutralizer diet helped clear up her skin problem. Within one month she had regained her beautiful skin.

Niacin (Vitamin B)

Niacin is part of the entire B complex series of vitamins. It is important in oxidizing the carbohydrates in a diet and helps build enzymes that give you sound mental health and youthful, healthy skin. Niacin is also thought to be important in the operation of the human brain and for the proper functioning of the nervous system.

When niacin is lacking in the human diet it can lead to nervous disorders that range from simple nervousness to insanity. Niacin also contributes to healthy hair growth through its effect on the blood's circulation to the scalp.

Most of the foods that contain niacin can be found in the calorie–neutralizer diet, including lean meats, liver, fish, poultry, bran and yeast. It is also found abundantly in the fiber-rich, green leafy vegetables that make up a large part of the diet.

LACK OF VITAMIN B MADE TV STAR
HIGHLY NERVOUS AND ERRATIC

One of the biggest stars in a popular TV series not only became 25 pounds overweight but he began drinking heavily and acting in a very erratic and nervous manner. People were afraid he was going to have a nervous breakdown.

One day I happened to visit him on the set and watched him work. He argued with his fellow workers, raged when his lines were changed and acted in a very hostile manner toward the director and his leading lady.

Later, when they had a lunch break and he went to his dressing room, I accompanied him and we talked over his problems. I had known him when he was a young actor on the way up, so he had faith in my advice and guidance from past experiences. He told me his story and I listened carefully before giving my advice.

As we talked, he drank several cocktails, smoked many cigarettes and paced nervously around the dressing room. Finally he stopped and asked, "Do you think I'm becoming mentally unbalanced, Norvell?"

I told him that I realized he was under a great strain, but so were other members of the company, so it had to be some other cause. I began to carefully check his diet to find out why he was so overweight. I soon discovered that his diet was totally wrong, and that he was actually suffering from vitamin deficiency, including niacin, cutting out many of the foods that would have given him B-1, as well as other B complex vitamins.

Our first step was to get him back to his normal weight. He was told to eat foods so rich in niacin that his symptoms would automatically begin to disappear in a short time. I included such foods as liver, lean meats, fish, poultry, bran, yeast, and leafy, green vegetables in his diet, and then scheduled his menus along the lines given in this book. For his drinking and excessive smoking I urged him to seek out competent help from a physician or psychologist.

This story has a happy ending, which many of his TV stories do not have, for he completely lost the 25 excess pounds within three weeks. His sustaining diet included all the B complex elements. He become a totally different person—more calm, more reasonable and more co-operative than he had been formerly.

Vitamin B-12

Vitamin B-12 was first isolated in 1948 and was then recommended in the treatment of pernicious anemia. It has since been found essential for the proper functioning of the body's metabolism.

This is very important when trying to lose weight, for it is the metabolism that burns up the calories. If it fails in its function those calories are turned into fat deposits. The new calorie–neutralizer diet helps this process of removing fat so it is important to include vitamin B-12 in the daily menus.

Vitamin B-12 increase mental alertness and physical vigor. As it contains cobalt, it is also essential to the normal functioning of bone marrow. When vitamin B-12 is lacking in the human diet it disturbs the nervous system and affects the enjoyment of sexual relations.

Many calorie–neutralizer foods are rich sources for this important vitamin. These include meat, milk, liver and organ meats. It can also be obtained in fish, eggs and milk products such as cottage cheese, buttermilk and yogurt.

LACK OF VITAMIN B-12 CAUSED HER TO BECOME ANEMIC

An example of how lack of proper nutrition can lead to health disturbances was the case of Rose L., 18. She had put on

25 pounds when she was 15 years old, and had never lost what her family called "baby fat."

The fact that Rose was anemic never surfaced until after she began the calorie–neutralizer diet to lose weight. When her doctor diagnosed her as being anemic, I realized that foods high in vitamin B-12 would have to be included in her diet.

Rose was given more fish in the reducing diet than I normally recommend to most dieters. For lunch she ate cottage cheese and boiled eggs. For dinner she had a 4-ounce serving of lean meat, with two of the reducing vegetables. She ate some plain yogurt and buttermilk for lunch or sometimes between meals, with salads.

Rose lost 25 pounds in a little more than three weeks. Normally I do not recommend buttermilk and yogurt for the average person trying to lose weight for they are too quickly digested and absorbed, but in Rose's case it was essential that she obtain large amounts of vitamin B-12 to help with her physical problem. When her doctor again performed tests he found that Rose's anemia had perceptibly improved.

FIVE OTHER B VITAMINS NEEDED IN THE DIET

There are other B vitamins that have been found to be needed in the human diet.

Pantothenic Acid

This form of the B complex affects the assimilation of carbohydrates and helps the metabolism. It has a strong effect on the adrenal glands, which secrete the hormone substance known as adrenalin.

Pantothenic acid is in many of the calorie–neutralizer foods, such as liver, kidneys, yeast, egg yolk, blackstrap molasses, rice bran, wheat bran, peas and peanuts.

Choline

Choline is another important part of the vitamin B complex family. It helps the body absorb fats and prevents fatty degeneration of the liver. The transmission of nerve impulses from the brain to the body's organs and muscles also depends on choline.

Many of our calorie–neutralizer foods contain choline, including egg yolk and legumes such as beans, lentils and soybean products. Whole-grain cereals, beef heart and green vegetables are rich sources of choline.

Inositol

Inositol combines with choline in the absorption of fatty foods. It also helps protect the liver. Inositol also helps the stomach pass food through the intestines through a process called peristalsis. You can obtain it in most meats, which are given in the new calorie–neutralizer diet, as well as in soybeans, citrus fruits and cereal brans.

Folic Acid

Folic acid helps build normal red blood cells and fights anemia. It also helps you overcome stress conditions and build antibodies to fight germ invasion of the body.

Folic acid can be found in many calorie–neutralizer foods, such as green leafy vegetables, whole-wheat, veal, beef, salmon, liver, kidneys and organ meats.

Biotin

This B complex vitamin helps the enzymes function properly in the body fluids and assists the respiratory system.

Biotin can be found in many calorie–neutralizer foods, such as vegetables, nuts, grains, egg yolk, yeast, milk, and molasses. Liver is also a good source of biotin.

Vitamin C

This important vitamin has functions other than helping build the body's immunity to colds and infections. Scientists now believe it is essential to the human diet and helps maintain the cartilage, bones and teeth in good condition. Vitamin C also helps the body's network of small blood vessels, veins and capillaries to function more efficiently. This is especially true for the aged who often have circulatory difficulties affecting the legs and feet, causing cramps, numbness and other symptoms.

Vitamin C cannot be stored in the body and must be supplied daily. Fortunately, in the calorie–neutralizer diet, many of the foods contain large quantities of vitamin C. Some of these are tomatoes, raw cabbage, green peppers, cauliflower, kale, parsley, watercress, broccoli, spinach, grapefruit, lemons, oranges, limes, raspberries and black currants. New potatoes are also rich in this vitamin.

Vitamin D

Vitamin D helps form strong bones and teeth. It assists the child in achieving normal body growth. This is one reason why whole milk is so essential in a growing child's diet. Vitamin D also helps the body absorb phosphorous and calcium and helps calm the nerves.

Vitamin D is called the "sunshine vitamin" because it is found abundantly in the sun's rays. It is found in many of the calorie–neutralizer foods such as milk, eggs, tuna, salmon, sardines, mackerel, and in irradiated yeast. It can also be obtained in fish liver oil capsules.

Vitamin E

Normal functioning of the cardiovascular system depends on Vitamin E. It is sometimes called the "sex" vitamin and thought to be important in maintaining sexual potency as well as for the proper functioning of the reproductive glands. When vitamin E is lacking in an animal's diet there is often a degeneration of the testicles. Now many physicians are treating impotence in men and frigidity in women with vitamin E. This vitamin also helps women eliminate hot flashes, excessive menstrual flow and backache during menopause. Vitamin E, when taken with vitamin A, is also found to protect against liver disorders, dry skin, persistent headaches, and hair and skin problems.

An abundance of vitamin E is included in our daily calorie–neutralizer reducing menus. It is found in its natural form in wheat germ oil and wheat germ, corn oil and corn germ, as well as soy oil, muscular meats, nuts, eggs, legumes and green leafy vegetables. Some green vegetable should be included each day, not only while reducing, but in the normal sustaining diet after losing the required weight.

LACK OF VITAMIN E IN DIET
CAUSED BETTE K. MANY PROBLEMS

For several years Bette K. weighed a normal 130 pounds. Then, for no apparent reason she began to gain weight and soon tipped the scales at 190 pounds. This situation went on for two years. Bette began to have irregularities in her monthly cycles, as well as backaches, headaches and painful cramps.

Bette also lost all sexual interest in her husband. It was so difficult for her to tolerate his sexual advances that she seriously considered getting a divorce. The couple had one child and this kept her from rushing into a separation or divorce.

Here was an overweight case that was so severe it undoubtedly produced some of the physical symptoms from which Bette suffered. Her doctor did not guess at the causes; although he told her she was overweight, he did not suggest any special diet.

In the dietary workshop we did not try to seek the causes of her being overweight or to diagnose her physical symptoms. We determined her present diet was principally one of high carbohydrates, fats and desserts.

It was fairly easy for Bette to go on the calorie–neutralizer diet, for we substituted foods that were low in calories and nonfattening for the high-calorie foods she had been eating. She could eat all she wanted each day of these low-calorie foods and still feel comfortably full.

Bette lost 10 pounds her first week on the new diet. The second week I began to substitute other foods that would help with her physical problems while continuing to help her lose weight.

For the next two weeks Bette began taking wheat germ in large quantities. Instead of ordinary meats, such as beef, pork and chicken, she ate muscular meats, brains, kidneys, hearts and liver, with plenty of green leafy vegetables. Also she had two eggs a day for breakfast, and lentils, lima beans and navy beans for dinner at least twice a week.

It took Bette seven weeks to lose the entire 60 pounds, but the improvements in her physical condition were so amazing that her doctor declared her miraculously improved. In addition, Bette regained sexual interest in her husband and no longer suffered from painful cramps or other symptoms even when she stopped dieting. She returned to her normal weight of 130 pounds and continued taking the calorie–neutralizer foods that were rich in vitamin E.

Vitamin F

Vitamin F helps absorb other vitamins and distribute calcium throughout the body. It contributes to general good health and normal growth. When vitamin F is lacking in the diet there is a tendency of arteriosclerosis. Vitamin F helps the body resist disease and maintain its proper cholesterol level.

Vitamin F can be obtained in such foods as peanuts, soybeans, sunflower oils, vegetable and grain oils, wheat germ, safflower and most grains. Wheat germ may be sprinkled over salads or in soups to add more of this important vitamin.

Vitamin K

Recent scientific research shows that vitamin K is important to the normal clotting of the blood and to prevent hemorrhages. It is believed also that vitamin K is important in human longevity.

Many of the vegetables in the priority no. 1 list of calorie–neutralizer foods contain sufficient quantities of this vitamin to satisfy the body's needs. It is found in spinach, cabbage, kale, tomatoes, soybeans, liver and vegetable oils. You can also obtain it from egg yolks and alfalfa.

Vitamin P

Vitamin P is thought to be essential to the normal health of the capillary system. It is also important to sexual arousal. Another important function of this vitamin is cell feeding and the removal of waste products from the body. Vitamin P gives the body protection from many different diseases and helps in the functioning of the body's vital organs.

Many of the calorie–neutralizer fruits and vegetables contain vitamin P, including prunes, plums, grapes, citrus fruits, spinach, parsley, green peppers, lettuce, cabbage, watercress, carrots and apples. This vitamin is also obtained from paprika.

CHAPTER 7

The Calorie–Neutralizer Extension Diet to Lose from 30 to 60 More Pounds

You have learned in preceding chapters how you can easily lose 10 to 25 pounds on the calorie–neutralizer diet. However, you may be one of those individuals who needs to shed from 30 to 60 pounds more. If this is true, there is the danger that such prolonged dieting can lead to monotony and even cause you to suspend dieting altogether.

To avoid this, I have worked out a system of calorie–neutralizer variation diets that will permit you to continue losing weight easily without suffering from hunger pangs or other distressing symptoms.

This extension diet still uses the calorie–neutralizer foods but they give a variety to your diet that makes it easy to continue for another month or two without giving up in despair.

HOW TO OVERCOME THE
MONOTONY OF PROLONGED DIETING

There is a certain monotony to sticking with a diet that features limited vegetables, fruits, grains and meats. This is especially true if no carbohydrates are used. After several weeks on such a diet, most people lose interest and "go off the wagon." The result is that they quickly put on the extra pounds they lost in the first week or two of the diet.

You can continue to lose 30 to 60 more pounds by using the extension diet. This will permit you to eat some foods that are richer in calories than those used in the first two or three weeks of your diet. In the extension diet you will also be permitted some carbohydrates in the form of desserts. They please your sweet tooth but are easily neutralized by certain combinations of vegetables in the second list of calorie–neutralizer foods.

ROMANTIC ACTOR LOST
40 POUNDS ON THIS EXTENSION DIET

Over a period of years, I have advised many of Hollywood's stars on career matters, including losing excess weight. At one Hollywood party I renewed the acquaintance of an aging romantic actor, whom I had known when he was a handsome, slender leading man. I was shocked to see how his jowls and fat paunch were detracting from his appearance. He was 40 pounds overweight and his popularity was slipping rapidly.

As we chatted about old times, he was drinking one cocktail after another, and eating appetizers from a tray that was being passed. These consisted of fattening pieces of sausage with bacon wrapped around them, cheeses on little crackers, stuffed mushrooms and other fattening goodies. Later, at dinner, he drank wine and gorged on steak, potatoes and creamed vegetables, followed by a heavy dessert of ice cream cake, with two cups of coffee and real cream, as well as two teaspoonfuls of sugar in each cup.

After dinner, when I registered my shock at his choice of fat foods at dinner, he wailed, "What can I do? I'm starved all the time, and the more weight I gain, the more hungry I seem to be."

I told him about my calorie–neutralizer diet, and he agreed to meet me the next day at the studio, where he was taking tests, to discuss the diet in detail. Let me tell you briefly how we handled his weight problem.

I first put him on the regular calorie–neutralizer diet, removing all carbohydrates from his daily menus. He also had to stop drinking any kind of alcohol. After two weeks he had lost 15 pounds, and was so encouraged that it was easy for him to go on the extension diet to lose 25 more pounds.

The first week of the extension diet I let him eat a heavy breakfast to sustain him in his heavy work schedule before the cameras. He usually had two eggs with bacon or sausage; occasionally he ate an omelet made with cheese, mushrooms or chopped-up ham. He had snacks in mid-morning of shrimp, tuna salad or chicken salad, with plenty of cucumbers, radishes, tomatoes, celery stalks and green peppers.

For dinner he could eat steak with a green salad and two of the calorie–neutralizer vegetables on the no. 2 list. For lunch and dinner he had fruit desserts, low-calorie puddings or stewed apples.

The first week on his extension diet he lost 10 pounds and never felt hungry or fatigued. He did not seem to miss the carbohydrates but he did occasionally take a cocktail before dinner.

After two weeks on the extension diet he shifted from meat to fish with all the calorie–neutralizer vegetables he wanted from both lists no. 1 and 2. Salads played a big part in his meals, for they slowed down the metabolic processes and kept him from absorbing too many calories from the heavy meals he ate. He still had big breakfasts and lunches that included shrimp salads, lobster and crabmeat. On one day he had a delicious seafood platter made up of four varieties of fish, including crab, lobster, shrimp and filet of sole. Despite the fact that he ate as many as 2000 calories a day, and sometimes more, he continued to lose weight on this diet. Finally, after another two weeks, he registered 7 and 8 pounds loss. The last 25 pounds were slower for there did not seem to be any real need to hasten the process. He was feeling well, looked better than ever and for photographic purposes it was best not to lose weight too rapidly, which would have given him a haggard appearance.

Within a six-week period this romantic actor once again became lean-jawed, his fat belly disappeared, and some moderate exercise in swimming and jogging helped firm up his flesh. In his next picture he once again became the handsome leading man his fans expected him to be. His career flourished from then on and he kept on the normal, sustaining diet given later in this book, never again having a weight problem.

CALORIE–NEUTRALIZER VEGETABLES TO ADD TO EXTENSION DIET

To give wider variety to the extension diet, you can add the following vegetables to your daily menus. These are also calorie–neutralizers but they have more fat calories than those given in priority list no. 1. You can have two servings of these vegetables with lunch or dinner, or you can select one vegetable from each list.

CALORIE–NEUTRALIZER VEGETABLE LIST NO. 2

artichokes	beets	parsnips
carrots	chives	red peppers
peas	white navy beans	eggplant
corn	onions	white potatoes
squash	rutabagas	lima beans

It is better to lose weight more slowly when you have 30 or more pounds to lose. Good nutrition is assured and you avoid flabbiness or a haggard appearance. You can have two servings of calorie–neutralizer vegetables from priority list no. 1 or two from the ones given above.

To add variety to the extension diet you can choose calorie–neutralizer fruits from the following list. These contain more carbohydrates than those in priority list no. 1, but they still fall in the acceptable limits of carbohydrates. This means you will not have more than 50 to 60 grams a day while you are reducing.

CALORIE–NEUTRALIZER FRUIT LIST NO. 2

peaches	pineapple	tangerines
apricots	plums	blackberries
nectarines	pears	raspberries
limes	cherries	loganberries
grapes	prunes	papaya

YOU CAN NOW BEGIN THE
FIRST PHASE OF YOUR EXTENSION DIET

Now that you understand the general plan for the extension diet you are ready to begin the first phase, which can assure you of losing weight each week, steadily and surely, while you remain on this diet.

THE FIRST WEEK OF YOUR EXTENSION DIET

For this important first week of your extension diet you can eat as much fish as you wish with two calorie–neutralizer vegetables. Use these in any combination you wish. For instance, the first day you might have broiled sea bass for lunch or dinner, with a beet salad and asparagus. Or, try peas and squash, or spinach and artichokes for your vegetables. For dessert you can have a low-calorie pudding of chocolate, lemon or butterscotch flavor, with artificial whipped cream. You may even have real cream with your coffee at breakfast, and real butter on your whole-wheat breakfast toast. These indulgences are permitted because they are neutralized by the other foods you are given, and also because your body still requires some fats for metabolizing the foods you eat.

On this fish diet for the one week, you can even eat fish twice a day, until your appetite is satisfied. This can be up to 1½ pounds. Select from the following list what you want for each day of your fish-and-vegetables extension diet week.

sea bass	lobster
halibut	crab
flounder	shrimp
salmon	shad roe
(canned salmon is permitted)	abalone
fresh tuna	trout
canned tuna	
(in water, not oil)	

A HEAVY BREAKFAST PERMITTED
DURING EXTENSION DIET

For breakfast all during this week you can have a wide variety of dishes, including bran cereal with cream, two eggs any style, three strips of bacon, one piece of protein or whole-wheat toast, with real butter and marmalade, and coffee or tea.

Breakfasts can be your most interesting and varied meals, for you can have such foods as chipped beef on whole-wheat toast and eggs Benedict with Canadian bacon. Some mornings you can have a cheese omelet, or eggs scrambled with chopped onions, pieces of ham and green pepper, or an omelet made with any of these ingredients: chicken livers, mushrooms or jelly. One or two mornings of the fish diet week you might try eating creamed tuna on whole-wheat toast, rather than cereal or eggs.

SEATTLE WOMAN
LOST 55 POUNDS ON
CALORIE–NEUTRALIZER·EXTENSION DIET

When people need to lose 50 or more pounds, I usually put them on the calorie–neutralizer extension diet immediately. I know that they may quickly tire of the monotony of the limited foods they can eat on the first diet. I usually substitute the low-caloried fish or meats with tomatoes or other vegetables for a couple of weeks. This achieves results and also keeps them from tiring of the diet.

An example of a person who benefited from the extension diet was Millie S. She lived in Seattle and came to a lecture I did there in a big theater. She was a fine-looking woman of about 45 but she weighed 195 pounds; her normal weight should have been closer to 135 pounds.

One of the main reasons why Millie wanted to lose weight was because her marriage of 20 years had floundered. Her husband had lost interest in her. As she had two grown children and a happy home otherwise, she felt his lack of interest in her might be because she had gained so much weight.

I put Millie on the extension calorie–neutralizer diet right away, for I realized her weight problem could not be solved in a mere two or three weeks. For the first week she ate lean meat and the calorie–neutralizer vegetables from both no. 1 and no. 2 lists. She lost 10 pounds that first week. On the second week she substituted fish for meat and had as many as four calorie–neutralizer vegetables a day, with some low-calorie desserts. The second week she lost only 8 pounds, but she was now encouraged to go on with her diet.

I returned three weeks later and found a very different woman from before awaited my arrival. She had lost 35 pounds in that three-week period and the 2 extra pounds she now was over her normal weight went quickly in two more days of the extension diet. When she had her final interview with me her happy husband accompanied her. He told me that Millie was now like the girl he had married years before, and they were going on their second honeymoon to Hawaii!

A VARIETY OF FISHES PERMITTED
ON CALORIE–NEUTRALIZER EXTENSION DIET

On some days, when you are on the fish-week extension diet, you can have two different types of fish, such as halibut for lunch and lobster or shrimp for dinner. The next day you might change to salmon for lunch and sea bass or oysters for dinner. Another day you might try a combination seafood platter, cold or hot, to add variety to your fish meals. Many people enjoy eating fish occasionally. This gives a welcome relief to the monotony of dieting too long on only vegetables and lean meats or chicken.

For desserts during your fish-dieting week you can use a variety of fruits given in either priority list no. 1 or 2. You might try pineapple for lunch (if canned, use the dietetic kind, without sugar). For dinner, have sliced peaches with real cream. For breakfast, eat papaya before your bran cereal, or have a whole orange or grapefruit. Eat the pulp, not just the juice. Fresh raspberries or blackberries in season may be eaten with a touch of honey and real cream, as a dessert or an in-between meal snack.

To keep from being hungry between meals, keep a plate of radishes, celery stalks, cucumbers and tomatoes where you can nibble on them several times a day. For a special treat fill the celery stalks with cream cheese or a spoonful of peanut butter.

During this special fish week eat all you want of cantaloupes, watermelon, honeydew melon, apples, strawberries, grapefruit, rhubarb or pumpkin. These fruits on the no. 1 priority list take more calories to digest than they give to the body.

SECOND WEEK OF EXTENSION DIET
TO LOSE THOSE EXTRA POUNDS

On the second week of the calorie–neutralizer extension diet, you can eat any of the low-calorie meats, having at least half a pound of meat twice a day. This will give you a total intake of 1 pound of rich protein food. This will satisfy your hunger-stat and yet let you continue to take fat off if the meat is eaten with the variety of calorie–neutralizer vegetables and fruits given a little later.

Following are the low-calorie meats you can use in the second week's extension diet:

ground lean meat	liver
filet mignon steak	sweetbreads
tenderloin steak	breast of lamb
T-bone steak	leg of lamb or lamb chops
pot roast	veal
roast beef	pork chops (broiled, not fried)

All meat, even lean ground beef, contains small quantities of fat. Fat adds calories but it is not a carbohydrate in the sense that sugars and starches are. Therefore, lean meat may add calories but will not put on extra weight.

However, if any meat is eaten in excess, say as much as 2 pounds a day, it will put on extra weight because you will be eating more calories than your body can handle. The calorie–neutralizer vegetables and fruits will assist your body in handling certain amounts of fat and rich calories because they neutralize them, but you cannot overeat any of the various recommended diet foods without suffering consequences.

For this all-meat diet week you can eat any of the following calorie–neutralizer vegetables, having as many as two portions to each meal, such as lunch and dinner:

tomatoes	string beans	carrots
spinach	cauliflower	Brussels sprouts
celery	green peppers	beets
lettuce	watercress	squash
cucumbers	broccoli	peas
mushrooms	turnips	onions
asparagus	zucchini	parsnips
artichokes		

For lunch you could have a 5-ounce serving of meat with a big salad made of cucumbers, lettuce, tomatoes and green peppers, and a low-calorie dressing. Your meat dish could be broiled liver, with a warm vegetable such as peas, carrots or asparagus. You can even add a tasty pudding for dessert. With all this food you still won't put on weight, for the calorie–neutralizers will reduce the caloric intake.

EXTENSION DIET CAN
INCLUDE MEAT TWICE A DAY

For breakfast some mornings, you can have some form of meat such as kidneys, bacon, sausage or chipped beef on toast. The bacon and sausage should have most of the fat cooked out of it to avoid extra calories. Eat a whole grapefruit or two oranges before breakfast, as this adds the extra calorie–neutralizer you need to reduce the rich calories in the breakfast. These will reduce the caloric intake by 50 percent.

A big dinner might consist of filet mignon or any other favorite steak, with two servings of calorie–neutralizer vegetables, such as mushrooms and cauliflower, peas and zucchini or Brussels sprouts and spinach or squash. Also, you can have your favorite salad with a low-calorie dressing to add other calorie–neutralizers to the dinner.

Another dinner for this meat-eating week might consist of pot roast or roast beef, asparagus, broccoli or spinach, or any other combination of two vegetables you desire. Another meal suggestion is two pork chops (broiled) with any two vegetables on lists no. 1 and 2.

During the two- or three-week period of your extension diet you can have a wide variety of meats, including chicken, turkey and roast duck, with two of the calorie–neutralizer vegetables.

These extension diets are not intended to be used as a steady diet, even after you have lost the required pounds. To have a balanced diet including proteins, carbohydrates and fats, there must be a combination of foods that make up what I call the normal, sustaining diet. This is given in Chapter 12.

TRY A ONE WEEK ALL-VEGETABLE VARIATION DIET

To add further variety to dieting for any extended period of time, for one full week try using only calorie–neutralizer vegetables, with desserts of fruits, gelatin, puddings and other nonfattening, dietetic canned desserts.

There are many tasty ways of preparing these calorie–neutralizer vegetables. You can use herbs, spices, condiments and sauces to pep up your vegetable dishes, and eat as many of these vegetables as you wish without gaining an ounce.

George Bernard Shaw was a vegetarian most of his life and he lived to a ripe old age. He wrote most of his plays after the age of 60.

Mahatma Gandhi of India observed a strict vegetarian diet during most of his life. He tried eating meat in his early years while at Oxford and reported that he felt sluggish, tired and was unable to work or study well. When he went on a strict vegetarian diet, not even eating eggs or milk products, fish or any kind of meat, he experienced the greatest benefits in health and energy. When Gandhi was assassinated at the age of 79, doctors claimed that his body was so healthy and well-preserved that he might have been a man in his 40s!

A VEGETARIAN WHO STILL BECAME 15 POUNDS OVERWEIGHT

Judy A. heard me extol the virtues of being a vegetarian at a lecture. She came to me and said, "I'm a vegetarian but I've recently begun to gain weight. I'm now 15 pounds too heavy, but according to your theory, if one eats vegetables and some milk products one should never gain weight."

I explained to Judy that many vegetables are heavy in carbohydrates and should be eaten sparingly. Also, the type of dressing used on salads and cooked vegetables determines how many fat calories they have. Judy then told me she was a great salad eater but she used a dressing made with olive oil and lemon juice, as she did not like vinegar.

"Salads are fine," I told Judy, "but olive oil and other heavy oils should be avoided, especially when you are trying to lose weight. Use some of the dressings that are tasty and low-calorie and you will have no further weight problem."

Another thing wrong with Judy's diet was that she had been eating spaghetti, beans, macaroni and white bread, all heavy in carbohydrates, so her intake was well over the 60 grams allowed in the normal diet. All those extra calories were turned into fat.

I told Judy she could satisfy her appetite by eating between meals such nonfattening vegetables as radishes, tomatoes, cucumbers, celery and green peppers. She was advised to keep a plate of these handy where she could nibble on them as between-meal snacks.

In addition to her vegetarian diet, and also to keep her from eating so many carbohydrates, I suggested that Judy add fish to her reducing diet at least twice a week. She did this, having shrimp or crabmeat salad for lunch, broiled fish for dinner, and some days a seafood platter served with calorie–neutralizer vegetables. Some days she ate brown rice with the vegetables. She had eaten white rice formerly, not knowing that this devitalized product added more carbohydrates than proteins, but in the brown rice she began to receive more proteins.

It was no problem for Judy to lose the entire 15 pounds in only two weeks. Then she went on the vegetarian diet, using the low-fat, calorie–neutralizer vegetables, which, when added to the milk products, nuts, legumes and some fish, gave her a perfectly balanced diet for maintaining her normal weight. For desserts she stuck to fruits, dates and figs, using the dessert recipes given in Chapter 8.

USE WIDE VARIETY OF VEGETABLES WHILE ON THIS VARIATION DIET

To vary your all-vegetable diet, you can select vegetables from the following long list. Prepare them by steaming them. Use the varied nonfattening dressings that are given in the section that deals with salad dressings, sauces and condiments.

VEGETABLES PERMITTED FOR YOUR ALL-VEGETABLE VARIATION DIET

cabbage	sauerkraut	cucumbers
broccoli	green peppers	string beans
mushrooms	celery	garlic
turnips	leeks	okra
tomatoes	radishes	spinach
lettuce	asparagus	watercress
cauliflower		Brussels sprouts

The following vegetables have more fat calories than the above, but you may use these in small quantities if you wish to continue the all-vegetable diet beyond the one-week period. This variation diet will assuredly make you lose weight more rapidly than the other diets, if you do not become too bored by the use of these vegetables.

beets	onions	avocados
squash	red peppers	lentils
rutabagas	chives	white potatoes
kale	artichokes	sweet potatoes
parsnips	peas	corn
lima or navy beans		

BE A VEGETARIAN OR A MEAT-EATER— THE CHOICE IS YOURS

The calorie–neutralizer vegetable and fruit diet for one full week is easy and most pleasant to follow. You can eat all the vegetables you wish each day, from the lists given. You need not worry about overeating these vegetables for your stomach will tell you when you have had enough. You will still be able to register a weight-loss during the vegetarian week, but if you feel the need of a little extra nourishment, drink a glass of orange juice for breakfast, eat two eggs, or eat any of the calorie-neutralizer fruits for breakfast or as desserts.

There are thousands of vegetarians who live on vegetables, fruits, nuts, grains, cheese and milk products such as buttermilk, yogurt, cottage cheese and whole milk. Some also eat fish occasionally, and they remain slender and in perfect health all their active, long lives.

HOW TO SPICE UP YOUR VEGETABLES TO MAKE THEM DELICIOUS

To give the calorie–neutralizer vegetables delicious flavor while on this variation diet, you can add herbs, onions, garlic and condiments to them. On some evenings you might also try a large baked potato with margarine or butter.

When you have finished with these variation diets for a period of from four to six weeks and have lost the extra pounds you want to lose, you may decide to go on a lacto-vegetarian diet for life. You need not worry about not getting sufficient proteins, for you can add milk, cheese, butter, cottage cheese, pot cheese, yogurt, nuts, grains and bran, as well as brown rice to your sustaining diet, and you will never again have a weight problem. You rarely see a fat vegetarian!

If you do choose the vegetarian way of life you will probably see your health vastly improved, as well as removing the dangers of heart disease and high blood pressure.

CHAPTER 8

Calorie–Neutralizer Desserts to Satisfy That Sweet Tooth While Losing Weight

One of the great joys in eating is the satisfaction that comes from having rich desserts with your meals. Unfortunately, most desserts are fattening, as they are in the form of starches and sugars that fall in the carbohydrate class of foods. These are the high-calorie foods that are most quickly converted into fat cells by the body's metabolism.

To make up for this lack of desserts, I have created some low-calorie, nonfattening recipes using calorie–neutralizer foods.

MOST DESSERTS ADD HUNDREDS OF EXTRA CALORIES TO A MEAL

Most people follow up a heavy protein and carbohydrate dinner with desserts that add hundreds of extra calories—fat calories which turn into deadly acid ash and then are stored in fat deposits all over the body. These desserts usually consist of pies, cakes, ice cream, cookies, rich pastries and sometimes, coffee with cream and sugar, followed by an after-dinner drink. Obviously no one can hope to indulge daily in such sweet tastes and lose weight, especially when the dinner itself probably contained more calories than are allowed for two days of strenuous activities.

Many people who eat the usual rich desserts gain from 10 to 50 pounds in a few months and then find it hard to break the habit of overeating fattening carbohydrates.

In using the following calorie–neutralizer foods to prepare your desserts you will be lessening your caloric intake. You can eat full meals consisting of high-protein meats, with two vegetables, and in addition, a low-calorie dessert that gives balance to your meal and satisfies your craving for sweets. Most of these desserts consist of calorie–neutralizer fruits, with nuts and honey or brown sugar for sweetening. Although both are high-caloried, there is no harm in using a little to sweeten the fruits used in the desserts. Remember that most of the fruits used in these low-calorie desserts are calorie–neutralizers, making it impossible for these desserts to turn into unwanted fat.

The following example of an uncontrolled appetite for sweets clearly points out the hazards of eating sweets while dieting.

SHE GAINED 60 POUNDS BY EATING
TOO MANY RICH DESSERTS

Virginia B. ate very little meat or vegetables at mealtime so she could have two different desserts. This habit continued for several years, and her weight continued to increase from her normal of 120 to 180 pounds. Virginia became alarmed and sought aid.

Virginia's carbohydrate habit of many years standing was much more serious than appeared at first. Not only did she eat very little meat but she liked French fried potatoes, creamy sauce on vegetables, and she often substituted chicken country style, for red-blooded meat. This meant the chicken was rolled in flour and then fried in deep fat. She ate chicken soup with dumplings, one of her favorites, and always fried her fish. She had pizza or lasagna once a week. For breakfast she often had pancakes with melted butter and heavy syrup. Several times a week she had cookies or cake with her ice cream or other sugar-heavy desserts.

It took some talking and experimenting to help Virginia break her carbohydrate habit. I told her to stand in front of her mirror and visualize her fat potential for the future—how she would look at 200 or 250 pounds in a short time—and to tell herself she could not let this happen. It worked. Within two months Virginia lost 60 pounds. The carbohydrate habit was forever broken, and she now has a good chance of remaining slender in the future.

You need not limit your desserts to those recipes given below. You may also use any of the following fruits in any combinations for desserts. They will continue to reduce you, for they are alkaline in their chemical effect on your body, and help reduce the fattening acid ash that often accumulates from too rich a meal.

peaches	apricots	strawberries
pears	currants	grapefruit
cherries	plums	raspberries
cantaloupe	papaya	grapes
apples	oranges	honeydew melon
bananas	nectarines	loganberries
blueberries	persimmons	guavas
blackberries	pineapple	rhubarb
watermelon	mangoes	tangerines

CALORIE-NEUTRALIZER FRUIT CUP

4 cups of cantaloupe or honeydew melon balls. You can also use these with watermelon balls to add color.
4 oranges cut into pieces
3 sliced bananas
1 tbs. honey
1 tsp. lemon juice
1/3 cup grated coconut
Grenadine

Mix the cantaloupe and other fruit balls together with the oranges and bananas; add honey and lemon juice. Top this with grated coconut and chill before serving. Add a touch of grenadine. This makes a very delicious and satisfying dessert after any heavy protein meal.

LOW-CALORIE APPLEWHIP DESSERT

4 cups of applesauce (homemade with honey or artificial sugar)
5 egg whites beaten until thick
1 tbs. lemon juice
2 tbs. pineapple juice
1/2 tsp. ground ginger
1 tbs. honey or brown sugar

Add honey to eggs as you beat them, then put in applesauce. Add pineapple and lemon juice to the mixture and pour into glasses. Keep in refrigerator until ready to serve. A touch of ground ginger on top can be added for garnishing before serving.

STRAWBERRY MOUSSE DELIGHT

4 cups of strawberries (fresh or frozen)
1 cup of yogurt
1/2 tsp. vanilla extract
1/2 tsp. almond extract
5 tsp. honey or artificial sweetener

Mix strawberries with the yogurt, add the vanilla and almond extracts with the honey. Mix in a bowl and then chill in the refrigerator for an hour. Serve in glass dessert dishes.

Before continuing with other calorie–neutralizer desserts, let me give a word of warning regarding overeating even these desserts. They are rich in calories and you must use them with caution. The following example of what rich desserts can do to a person is from my files in the diet workshop.

HENRY J. DEVELOPED SYMPTOMS OF DIABETES AND GAINED 90 POUNDS BY OVEREATING SWEETS AND CARBOHYDRATES

When Henry J. tipped the scales at 250 pounds, he began to notice strange symptoms that alarmed him. His normal weight had been 160 pounds for years, but his love of high-calorie desserts, sugars, starches and creamy desserts finally took their toll. He began to suffer from excessive fatigue, terrific thirst and an uncontrolled appetite, which drove him to eat at night. Sometimes he would consume a quart of ice cream, and then finish up with half a chocolate cake. He drank water every half hour or so, and had a constant thirst, with frequent bouts of urination, at the most inconvenient times.

After he had a severe attack of dizziness and nearly fell down, he decided to see a doctor. The physician found that Henry was suffering from diabetes, and began the treatment for that condition. Of course, the doctor told Henry he would have to lose weight, or other symptoms, such as high blood pressure and heart trouble, might develop. As Henry was only 55 years old, with a wife and three children, the thought of something happening to him made him suddenly become serious about losing his excess weight.

Henry told me he was afraid to try a diet, for fear he would revert to his old habits again, and overdo on the sweets and carbohydrates.

Knowing Henry's physical condition, I told him to check our diet with his personal physician, to be sure there was nothing in it that would prove harmful. Henry did. He was given the green light by his doctor, when he learned the reducing menus and the calorie–neutralizer methods.

I realized that Henry's weight loss must be more gradual than in most cases, so I scheduled a weight loss of about 5 to 8 pounds a week, allowing him plenty of foods to meet his huge appetite. Fruits were kept to a minimum, because of their sugar content, but fruits like apples and cantaloupes he could eat all he wanted.

Henry ate meat twice a day, for lunch and dinner. Eggs were included in his breakfast menus, with sausage and bacon three or four times a week. White bread was cut out and protein and whole-wheat bread were substituted. He ate only one slice a day. As Henry loved beef in any form, he had plenty of roast beef, steaks, veal chops, lamb chops, chicken and turkey. Fish was also included in his diet once or twice a week. Plenty of between-meal snacks were allowed, consisting of calorie–neutralizer vegetables, such as celery, cucumbers, radishes, tomatoes and lettuce, as well as cheeses, yogurt and buttermik. Whole milk was removed from his diet, but he occasionally ate cottage cheese made from low-fat milk.

On this rather heavy protein, vegetable and fruit diet, Henry was able to steadily lose 5 to 8 pounds a week. It took him a little more than three months to lose his 90 pounds, but the results in benefits to his health and his appearance were amazing. Henry's doctor checked on his blood pressure and heart at the end of the three months and found them excellent.

CANTALOUPE ROYALE

This is a delicious dessert to serve after a meat or fish dinner. It gives the impression you are feasting like royalty and yet adds very few calories.

3 bananas
8 tbs. sour cream
3 tsp. honey
2 cantaloupes

Cut the peeled cantaloupe into 1-inch cubes. Mash the bananas into a bowl and add honey and sour cream. Mix until thoroughly blended. Put the pieces of cantaloupe into the mixture and toss. When serving, be sure that the sour cream covers all the fruit thoroughly.

CRÈME DE MENTHE PINEAPPLE JOY

4 tsp. grated coconut
several slices of pineapple, canned or fresh
4 tbs. crème de menthe
4 tsp. grated ginger

Use either chunks or slices of pineapple. Place in a dessert dish and sprinkle with crème de menthe. Sprinkle grated coconut and ginger on top. If available, garnish with fresh mint leaves and serve cold. The exotic flavor given by the crème de menthe will make your guests feel they are enjoying a wicked dessert, yet it is simple and nonfattening.

EGYPTIAN FRUIT DELIGHT

This dessert is made of dates, figs and almonds. It is somewhat higher in calorie-count but not enough to keep you from still reducing while eating a regular calorie–neutralizer meal of salads and meat.

Combine a dozen or more pitted dates, figs and almonds,

(chopped) with shredded coconut and a tablespoonful of honey. Put the ingredients into a bowl and mix together. This will make a generous supply of this dessert. Shape into little pyramids to make them more attractive and put them into the refrigerator until ready to use. You may serve them as an after-dinner dessert or keep them indefinitely and use them for in-between snacks.

FRUIT-COCONUT COMBO SURPRISE

4 ripe bananas
6 peach halves (fresh or canned)
6 pear halves (fresh or canned)
1 cup raisins (soaked until soft)
3 cups of canned blackberries or raspberries (or use frozen)
1/4 cup shredded coconut

Line a pie tin with a layer of crumbled graham crackers. Put a layer of sliced bananas, a layer of pears and a layer of peaches over the crackers. Sprinkle with coconut and add a bit of shredded ginger.

Top this with artificial whipped cream or use a cupful of yogurt or sour cream. Chill in the refrigerator before serving.

ORANGE SUPREME

This simple dessert is easy to make but it gives an exotic look to your after-dinner desserts. All you need for this are:

5 oranges (sliced thin)
2/3 cups of shredded coconut

On top of a layer of sliced oranges sprinkle coconut. Continue the process, with a layer of oranges topped with the coconut, making several layers. Sprinkle chopped nuts on top and chill before serving.

You may use other fruits for this dessert, or a combination of fruits, to give the impression you are having a sweet dessert at the end of your meal. The calories contained in these various fruits are few. Here are some fruits you can combine:

• Pears, either canned or fresh.
• Take a can of grapefruit sections and combine with canned peach halves. Serve in a sherbet dish.
• Try a combination of apple, grapefruit and orange slices. Mix together in a glass sherbet dish and chill before serving.

• Another variation: use a can of black Bing cherries and a can of purple plums. Mix together and chill.

• Combine various types of melons in season. Use equal balls of honeydew, Persian, cantaloupe and watermelon, mixing them together. Put a dash of grenadine on each dish you serve. Another good combination is made with cantaloupe and Bing cherries, or with purple plums and cantaloupe. You can also make one with diced oranges and honeydew melon.

BANANA SPLENDOR

6 or 7 bananas
3 tbs. brown sugar or honey
1/2 tsp. cinnamon
1 tsp. ground ginger
3 tbs. margarine or butter
1/2 pound creamed cheese
1 cup plain yogurt

Brown the halved bananas over a low fire slightly in margarine. Put 6 halves of the bananas into a buttered pie plate. Mix brown sugar or honey with the cream cheese and the cinnamon. Spread half of the mixture over the 6 banana halves. Then put the remaining bananas on top and spread with the balance of the mixture. Top this with the yogurt and place in an oven for 20 minutes at 350 degrees. This should serve six people.

APRICOT BOUQUET

One of the most popular fruits in the Middle East and Far East is the golden apricot. Many legendary stories are told about its virtues, and in recent days miracle healing powers have been claimed by some from the apricot's pits. This delicious fruit is a fine calorie–neutralizer as it is alkaline in its effect on acid ash.

10 or 12 whole apricots (dried or canned may be used also)
7 egg whites, beaten stiff
1/4 tsp. artificial salt
5 tbs. honey or brown sugar
1/4 tsp. almond extract

Shred the apricots in a blender until they are pulp. Beat the egg whites until firm. Put the apricots into the blender with the eggs and other ingredients. Cook in a greased double boiler for half an hour.

Serve Apricot Bouquet with pineapple or grape juice as a sauce. Or, top it with artificial whipped cream, a spoonful of sour cream or yogurt.

Although as a general practice in our calorie–neutralizer reducing diet I do not recommend drinking fruit or vegetable juices, there are times when it can be recommended, for the juices are alkaline in nature and make an excellent drink to satisfy your taste buds when you are hungry between meals.

FRUIT JUICE ELIXIR

Mix together equal parts of cranberry, pineapple and apricot juice. Add the juice of half a lemon. Cool and serve. This is delicious and refreshing, especially on a hot summer day.

You may also combine various juices to suit your taste, using apple cider, lemon, grapefruit, orange, grape juice or peach. Pineapple juice mixes quite well with all of these juices and is a very satisfying, cooling drink between meals if hungry.

When you have lost the required weight and can eat all things in moderation you can sometimes go on a fruit and vegetable juice cleansing diet. This is when you drink various fruit and vegetable juices for an entire day. These are quickly absorbed by the body, and should only be done on occasion. However, many people believe in using carrot, celery, beet, watercress, spinach and cabbage juice as a daily routine, drinking a glass once a day. There is no harm in such a practice, if one is of normal weight, for the calorie–neutralizer fruits and vegetables are highly desirable whether in the form of juices or eaten raw.

BANANA HONEY FLOAT

Although bananas are high in carbohydrates they are an excellent food and can be eaten at least once a day when you are on your normal, sustaining diet. Your body requires about 60 grams of carbohydrates normally, when not dieting; you can have as high as 45 grams of carbohydrates a day while dieting.

Banana Honey Float will add a festive touch to your dinner and make your guests think it is a rich dessert.

4 sliced bananas
4 tsp. lemon juice
4 egg whites, unbeaten
2 spoonfuls honey
2 tsp. vanilla
nutmeg or cinnamon for topping

Thoroughly mash the bananas and lemon juice together. Add the egg whites, a touch of sea salt and the honey and vanilla. Blend together in the blender or by hand until thoroughly mixed. Pour into sherbet glasses and top with a touch of cinnamon or nutmeg. Cool and serve.

PAPAYA À LA WAIKIKI

The papaya is a delicious tropical fruit that flourishes in the lush atmosphere of Hawaii. I was first served this delicious dessert at the home of a couple who lived near Waikiki beach in Honolulu and received the recipe from the charming hostess. Papaya is a very tasty and nourishing fruit even when eaten by itself as a breakfast dish or as a dessert at any meal. However, if you want a rich tasting dessert you can prepare it in this way.

Cut a papaya in half. Chop together several dried prunes, apricots and dates (the pitted type). Add some chopped nuts and two teaspoonfuls of honey. Mix these ingredients together, then stuff the halves of papaya with this mixture. Top each dish with yogurt when you serve it.

This makes an excellent dessert after a light luncheon of chicken salad, tuna salad or a chef's salad with a big mixture of fresh, green calorie–neutralizer vegetables. You can also serve it as a main dish with a slice of date-nut bread.

MAGNOLIA CUSTARD RICE PUDDING

1/2 cup of rice (the quick-cooking white rice is all right. If you want more, double the entire recipe.)
1/4 cup brown sugar (or four tbs. honey if preferred)
2 tbs. plain gelatin
1 tsp. almond extract
4 cups milk
4 tbs. water
1 tsp. vanilla
1 cup whipped cream (artificial kind)

Prepare the rice in a double boiler, until tender. If you use the quick-cooking white rice, this can be prepared easily in a few moments. Before you add the brown sugar or honey and gelatin, soak them in cold water for about four minutes, so the gelatin will become thoroughly soft and saturated with the honey or sugar. Let this stand until ready to use, then stir in the almond extract and the vanilla flavoring. Chill in the refrigerator until ready to serve. Top with artificial whipped cream before serving.

CALORIE–NEUTRALIZER FRUIT MEDLEY

The following dessert utilizes the calorie–neutralizer fruits that can be eaten with any meal without fear of adding extra calories. When these fruits are in season they can be used fresh, but you may also use canned fruits, especially if you buy the dietetic kind, free of sugar. If you use fresh fruits, peel the peaches, apricots and plums before using them.

6 peaches
6 apricots
6 ripe or canned plums
2 tbs. honey
5 tbs. lime or lemon juice
3 tsp. pineapple juice

Slice the peaches, apricots and plums. Mix the honey and lime and pineapple juice and pour over the fruit. When ready to serve as an after-dinner dessert you can top the fruits with lemon, orange, pineapple or raspberry sherbet. Serve in glass sherbet dishes. They add a festive, colorful touch to any dinner or luncheon.

PRELUDE-TO-LOVE AMBROSIA

This delicious dessert drink may be served hot or cold in sherbet glasses. It is stimulating to the emotions and makes a good sweet drink to satisfy the taste buds after a hearty meat protein or fish meal.

4 tbs. of honey
4 egg yolks
4 tbs. of red wine

Beat ingredients together until thoroughly blended. Put the mixture into a pan and apply medium heat until it begins to boil, then turn off the heat. Be sure that you continue to beat the mixture constantly while it is cooking, until it is quite fluffy and thick. Refrigerate until cool, after pouring it into glass sherbet dishes, then serve.

GOLDEN APRICOT TARTS

Use fresh apricots if possible for this satisfying dessert. If not in season, use dried apricots. Soak them overnight until they are soft and full. Take one pound of apricots and cut them in halves. Place in a whole-wheat crust. Blend together the following ingredients:

2 cups whole-wheat flour
1 cup sour cream
1 tsp. brown sugar or honey
1 cake of yeast
1/4 lb. of margarine

Blend together the sugar or honey and the yeast with the sour cream, until it is a thick paste. Let the mixture rise for about an hour.

You can mix sea salt or artificial salt with the margarine, if you do not use ordinary table salt. Add the sour cream to the mixture and knead in a bowl. If you find the dough sticks to the pan add more flour until it is easy to handle. Now roll the dough into a thin pie crust and line the bottom of a pie plate. If you wish to make individual tarts, prepare smaller pans to receive the apricots.

Top the apricots with yogurt, which you can blend with a tablespoon of honey. Bake 30 minutes in an oven heated to 340 degrees.

You can count on these calorie–neutralizer desserts to give you pick-up energy without adding extra fat. In fact, they lessen caloric intake of the rich foods eaten at any particular meal, for the fruits used are all in the alkaline reaction class. They help neutralize the harmful acid ash accumulations that lead to fat deposits in your body.

CHAPTER 9

Add Pleasure
to Your Dieting with
Calorie–Neutralizer Salads

Dieting should never become a dull, boring routine, in which you consume tasteless foods because you have to lose weight. The pleasure you get from foods can continue by having a wide variety of salads and dressings to make them more delicious. There are many combinations of nourishing yet slenderizing calorie–neutralizer vegetables that give you bulky fiber and keep you from becoming too hungry while dieting.

You can also spice up your reducing menus by using flavorful salad dressings, sauces, marinades and low-calorie mayonnaise. These are all tasty but extremely low in calories. There are many low-calorie salad dressings on the market that are excellent and may be used. However, you can create your own tasty low-calorie dressings. These can be kept in your refrigerator and used when needed.

The calorie–neutralizer salads furnish the body with tasty and nourishing vegetables, and at the same time act to help neutralize the calories eaten in any rich protein meal. You can even use these salads as the main dish of a luncheon or dinner. Add fruits, cheeses, meats, and fish, including shrimps, crab and lobster. Salads also can be used before a big meal to keep you from overeating calorie-rich foods, like proteins or carbohydrates. Salads can furnish your body with important vitamins and minerals that are needed in any balanced diet.

USE RAW VEGETABLES WHENEVER POSSIBLE FOR SALADS

Try to use raw vegetables as much as possible in all your salads, and use fruits that are in season. If you cannot get fresh fruits, used canned fruits such as apricots, pineapple, peaches, pears, cherries and frozen strawberries or raspberries. Wash off the heavy syrup or use the dietetic canned fruits that are made with artificial sugar.

Here are a few combination salads you may make using fresh vegetables. These calorie–neutralizer vegetables can be eaten as a main dish or to offset any heavy protein meat dish.

CUCUMBER AND BEAN SALAD

3 cucumbers, sliced
2 pounds of green snap beans
2-1/2 cups of water, artificial salt to taste (boil water)
1/3 tsp. black pepper
3 cups sour cream
3 tbsp. lemon juice

Cook the beans for about eight minutes; drain and cool. Mix together sour cream, pepper and lemon juice. Let stand one hour. Mix together the cucumbers, beans and dressing. Let this stand in the refrigerator an hour before serving.

FRESH CORN AND LIMA BEAN SALAD

Fresh or canned lima beans and corn
1 lb. of lima beans
1 lb. of corn kernels
2 cucumbers
2 fresh tomatoes
2 green peppers
half a head of lettuce

Cut up cucumbers, tomatoes and green peppers. Place on a bed of lettuce in a big salad bowl and use low-calorie French or Russian dressing.

COTTAGE CHEESE AND VEGETABLE SALAD

Use low-calorie cottage cheese for this salad. It may be served as the main luncheon dish, or a small portion with a protein meal.

1 head iceberg lettuce
10 or 12 spinach leaves
several stalks watercress
2 ripe tomatoes
2 cucumbers, sliced
1 container cottage or pot cheese

Shred the lettuce, chop up and add the spinach and watercress leaves. Combine the tomatoes and cucumbers, and serve with low-calorie dressings.

LETTUCE-TOMATO SALAD WITH GARLIC DRESSING

1 head lettuce
celery and spinach leaves, chopped up
2 or 3 tomatoes
2 sliced cucumbers

Make garlic dressing by combining juice of lemon with crushed garlic and a little vegetable or olive oil. Mix well and pour over salad. Serve cold.

CARROT, CABBAGE AND BEET SALAD

6 chopped carrots
6 chopped raw beets
1/2 head small cabbage
salad greens, lettuce, celery, green peppers, cucumbers

Chop up carrots, cabbage and beets. Add salad greens in a big bowl and mix thoroughly. Serve with a low-calorie dressing before a fish or meat dinner.

As these vegetables are all calorie–neutralizers, you can eat a very rich protein dinner with some sweet dessert and the salad will help neutralize the calories. You will still lose weight after eating what seems like a high-calorie, rich dinner.

SPECIAL AVOCADO CALORIE–NEUTRALIZER SALAD

Although no one would ever dare suggest eating avocados while reducing, you can occasionally enjoy this delicious fruit, for it is eaten with enough calorie–neutralizer vegetables to help reduce the caloric content of the avocado. This can be eaten for a complete lunch at times. Add protein by using boiled, cold shrimp, crab meat or lobster, with a low-calorie dressing.

Instead of eating the avocado out of the shell, cut it up and add celery, green peppers, onions and serve it on a bed of shredded lettuce. Be sure the avocado is soft and ripe. Mix the cold shrimp, crab meat or lobster with the cut-up avocado and vegetables. Serve cold with suitable dressing.

SALADS HELPED DELLA J.
LOSE 30 POUNDS IN THREE WEEKS

Many times an overweight person begins to suffer from symptoms that make them seek medical aid. Their aim is not so much to lose weight, which could be causing their physical problems, but to relieve the distressing symptoms.

Such was the case with Della J., who was 30 pounds overweight. She began to have strange feelings in her body, with erratic heart beat and distressing symptoms. Her doctor found that Della's blood pressure was higher than it should be. There was some evidence of sugar in the blood, which the doctor said could have come from wrong dietary habits. He began treatment for her condition but did not prescribe any special diet to lose the excess pounds.

Della came into the diet workshop to see if we could help her lose weight. She had been a heavy eater of fat meats, especially pork and roast beef. For lunches she had creamed chicken or chicken salad with rich mayonnaise, or sometimes cold lamb with potato salad, also heavy with mayonnaise. Her desserts were always the rich, fattening kind made with plenty of cream, butter and white flour. She had very few salads in her daily menus.

I included meats twice a day in Della's case because she could hardly visualize a meal without some form of meat. In her breakfast menus I included plenty of sausage, bacon and ham with her eggs, being sure that all the fat was taken out of the meats. Some mornings she had creamed beef on whole-wheat toast; other times, eggs Benedict, with ham and Béarnaise sauce. If she had been forced to cut out all rich foods at once, it is doubtful Della would have stayed with the diet more than one week.

Twice a day I included combination salads, such as those given in these recipes, with low-calorie dressings. Della felt that she was really not on a diet but actually eating normal meals.

Della lost 8 pounds in the first week. In the second week, when she began to have salads for lunch, and also for dinner, she lost 10 more pounds. The third week she lost the last 12 pounds of the 30 she wanted to lose.

Della went on the sustaining diet after the third week. She checked with her doctor, who found her blood pressure back to normal and the other symptoms subsiding. It is doubtful if Della will ever gain weight again. With the calorie–neutralizer, sustaining diet, she can have rich foods with plenty of salads and tasty dressings. This gives her enough variety so she need never again crave high-calorie carbohydrates and fats.

ASPARAGUS AND GRAPEFRUIT SALAD

2 lbs. of fresh, cooked asparagus (Canned asparagus will also do.)
2 grapefruits
mixed salad greens, lettuce, celery, green peppers, cucumbers

Cut grapefruit into segments, removing seeds. Put asparagus stalks on individual plates, which have a bedding of salad greens. Use five or six stalks of asparagus on each plate. Arrange slices of grapefruit to alternate with asparagus. Cut green pepper into strips, place alongside asparagus or across it. Add special dressing and serve.

All these vegetables are on the list of calorie–neutralizer foods and will give fiber bulk and also act as catalysts to reduce calories from meat dish or a dessert.

PEAR, PEPPER AND CHICORY SALAD

1/2 dozen pears, quartered (fresh or canned)
fresh, chopped up chicory
2 green peppers sliced into thin strips

Serve on a bed of lettuce with a low-calorie dressing.

BEAN SPROUT SALAD

1 cup bean sprouts
1/4 cucumber, diced
1/2 cup chutney sauce
1 cup pineapple chunks

Garnish with sliced tomatoes and halves of hard-boiled eggs. Decorate the salad bowl with strips of red pimentos or red and green peppers. Put these ingredients into the bowl of basic lettuce salad and serve with dressing of your choice.

CALORIE–NEUTRALIZER TOMATO SALADS

You can add great eye and taste appeal to any meal by using the delicious calorie–neutralizer tomato as a basis for salads. Stuff tomatoes with a variety of foods, such as crab, shrimp, chopped lobster tails, creamed mushrooms, hard-boiled eggs, cream cheese, chopped nuts and nut-meat mixtures.

Cut the tops off the ripe tomatoes and take out the center pulp. Blend it with any of the above ingredients and serve with a low-calorie dressing of your choice. This can become a whole luncheon meal, or a dinner dish on a warm summer's evening.

DATE, GINGER AND BANANA SALAD

Serve the following ingredients on a bed of lettuce: quartered bananas, cut up lengthwise; dates, pitted type; artificial whipped cream dressing. Sprinkle lightly with shredded ginger and serve cold for an appetizing luncheon dish.

Both bananas and dates are high carbohydrates, but when served with calorie–neutralizer lettuce, you can eat this salad without fear of adding weight.

EXCESSIVE HIGH-CALORIE
SALAD DRESSINGS ADDED WEIGHT

The use of excessive salad dressings, high in calories, can contribute to rapid weight gains. This happened to Martha G., who had gained weight alarmingly while on another diet to lose 39 pounds. When her weight shot up to 55 pounds more than normal she gave up her diet and came into the workshop to see what was wrong.

I checked on Martha's food intake and found that she was eating 50 percent carbohydrate foods. Much of this was in the form of rich salad oil dressings. Salads were the mainstay of her diet. She cut out all protein meats, depending on milk, cheese and yogurt for the proteins in her diet. I instantly removed the whole milk and, in addition to the calorie–neutralizer vegetables and fruits, gave her low-calorie cottage cheese and skimmed milk, with two salads a day. She was also permitted to have lean meat, chicken and fish with the salads. However, for a salad dressing, I gave her only low-calorie ones that were neutralized by the high-fiber, calorie–neutralizer vegetables making up the raw salads. Some of the ingredients in these salads were watercress, lettuce, green peppers, mushrooms, carrots and spinach leaves. By eating plenty of these low-calorie vegetables, she felt full at all times and lost her craving for rich carbohydrates, fats, oils and sweet desserts.

Martha registered a weight loss of 10 to 12 pounds a week on this high-salad diet, and the entire 55 pounds disappeared in a little more than five weeks.

CREAM CHEESE AND PINEAPPLE SALAD

This can be served as a complete luncheon dish with two slices of date-nut or whole-wheat bread.

Place several pineapple slices on a bed of lettuce and heap cream cheese on the leaves. Sprinkle finely ground nuts over it. No salad dressing is required for this.

FOUR DIFFERENT SALADS
YOU CAN MAKE FROM COLESLAW

Cabbage is one of the highest forms of the calorie–neutralizer vegetables when eaten raw. It should be included in the diet whenever possible while reducing. It has bulk and high fiber content and gives valuable nutrients to any diet. To cook cabbage destroys part of its mineral and vitamin content, so it is best to serve it in the form of coleslaw.

To prepare coleslaw use a slaw cutter or a very sharp knife to shred the cabbage. If you have a modern vegetable cutting machine use that to make the cabbage fine enough to eat without effort. Use only tender, inner leaves. Wash the cabbage first, then shred it, adding minced onion, some shredded carrot and a few parsley sprigs. You can use 3/4 cup of a low fat dressing made up of low-calorie mayonnaise, artificial sugar, vinegar, canned evaporated milk or real cream, and mix it to suit your taste.

PINEAPPLE COLESLAW

Use the basic coleslaw (minus the onion) to which you add 1 cup of shredded canned pineapple. If fresh pineapple is available use that. If not, use canned pineapple that is cooked in its own juice without added sugar.

APPLE COLESLAW

Chop up 2 or 3 large apples, remove the skin and cut up 2 red pimentos. Add this to the basic coleslaw and mix thoroughly.

ORANGE COLESLAW

Cut up 2 or 3 oranges into segments, then divide into smaller pieces. Add the oranges to the basic coleslaw, but do not add the onions.

CUCUMBER COLESLAW

Use 1 large cucumber, chop it up and add to the basic coleslaw. Onion is optional.

APPLE, RAISIN AND WALNUT SALAD

This salad uses various calorie–neutralizer foods that will help reduce the caloric intake of other foods, if eaten with a protein meal, or it may be used as a heavy midday luncheon dish.

Use a large salad bowl, into which you rub a cut clove of garlic. If you prefer, you may use half a spoonful of garlic powder or garlic salt. Add a teaspoon of mustard and 1 tablespoon of salad oil. Stir the oil and mustard together; add 2 tablespoons of lemon juice and blend together.

Now add cut-up lettuce leaves, uncooked peas, cut-up carrots, tomatoes and watercress. Prepare 2 or 3 hard-boiled eggs for garnishing. Add to this basic salad shredded white cabbage, chopped apples, seedless raisins and chopped walnuts. Mix the salad with your favorite low-calorie dressing and serve crisp and cold.

DELICATESSEN-STYLE CHOPPED VEGETABLES AND CREAM

This simple salad uses all calorie–neutralizer vegetables raw and flavored with sour cream. The dressing is rich in calories but remember, it will not give the body too many calories when you use these vegetables, for they take more energy to digest than they give to your body.

Chop up green onions, cucumbers, green peppers, celery stalks, watercress and radishes. Use a generous portion of sour cream on it and mix thoroughly. Serve cold with some form of crisp crackers or zwieback toast.

CHICKEN SALAD DELIGHT

For a full luncheon meal you can prepare leftover chicken or specially boiled chicken as a delicious cold salad with a low-calorie mayonnaise dressing. It can also be used as a between-meal snack.

1 whole boiled chicken (remove skin before boiling)
10 pimento-stuffed green olives
4 chopped sweet pickles
1/2 cup chopped celery
4 hard-boiled eggs
1 cup of low-calorie mayonnaise

Cut up the chicken into small pieces and add chopped celery, olives and sweet pickles. Chop up the eggs and add to mixture. Put in the mayonnaise and mix thoroughly. Use artificial salt. Put a lettuce bed on individual plates to serve.

An important part of any reducing diet is to be sure that foods do not become monotonous. This is especially true of salads, for if eaten without some kind of dressing they become unappetizing. The old formula for losing weight of cottage cheese and lettuce, fortunately, no longer applies. In the new calorie–neutralizer diet you can add rich-tasting salad dressings and sauces that make every meal a gourmet's delight.

SOUR CREAM DRESSING

Sour cream is rich in calories, but its flavor is so appealing that it can be used on many different salads without fearing that it adds extra calories. Remember, most of the vegetables used in our salads are calorie–neutralizers.

Combine 2 cups of sour cream
3 tbs. lemon juice
1/2 tsp. red pepper

SOUR CREAM SAUCE

This sour cream sauce can be used over fresh vegetable or fruit salads.

2 cups of diet cottage cheese
1/2 cup buttermilk
1/2 teaspoon lemon juice
artificial salt

HORSERADISH SAUCE

This is good to serve with lean meats or for various types of fish. To the above sour cream sauce add 2 tablespoons of white or red horseradish. This becomes a delicious sauce for any meat dish.

FRENCH DRESSING

You can make enough of this dietetic salad dressing to fill a large bottle. Kept in the refrigerator it will last a long time. Double the recipe if you wish to make more.

1 cup of tomato juice
1/4 tsp. garlic powder
1 cup wine or tarragon vinegar
1/2 tsp. dry mustard
1/2 tsp. oregano
artificial sugar to taste
artificial salt
a touch of black pepper

Combine the above ingredients in a glass jar and shake thoroughly before storing in the refrigerator.

VINAIGRETTE SAUCE

2 cloves of minced or diced garlic
4 tbs. water
1 tsp. herbs (tarragon, rosemary, thyme, dill)
1/4 tsp. paprika
a touch of artificial sweetener

Shake together in a glass jar and refrigerate until ready to use.

CHEESE SAUCE

1/2 cup buttermilk
1/2 lb. farmer cheese
1 egg yolk
1/2 tsp. paprika
2 tbs. lemon juice
salt and pepper to taste

Prepare this sauce in a double boiler. Melt the cheese and mix with the buttermilk, then put in the egg yolk and blend thoroughly in a blender. Add the paprika, salt, pepper and lemon juice.

This sauce can be used with all kinds of vegetables. It is especially delicious poured over cooked cauliflower or broccoli. Sprinkle Parmesan cheese over it and cook in a low oven for 30 minutes, letting the sauce gently permeate the vegetables.

BLUE CHEESE DRESSING

1 container of cottage cheese (low-fat may be used)
4 tbs. vinegar
4 tbs. water
2 envelopes (8 oz.) of blue cheese salad dressing mix (cut up blue
    cheese or Roquefort chunks, if you prefer)

Mix the above ingredients in a blender and store in a glass jar in the refrigerator. If you wish to make more, double the above quantities.

BÉARNAISE SAUCE

4 egg yolks
1/3 cup wine vinegar
2/3 cups margarine
2 tbsp. chopped scallions

1 cup white wine
1-1/2 tsp. cornstarch
salt and pepper to taste

Put vinegar, wine, scallions, pepper and salt into pan and bring it to a boil, but do not overcook. When mixture has evaporated somewhat, add a little wine and cornstarch in a cup and mix thoroughly. Add this to the above boiled mixture and let thicken.

Mix egg yolks with a little boiling water and add to above while it boils in a separate pan. Add butter slowly to this mixture as it simmers slowly; then add salt and pepper. Keep sauce warm before using it.

MUSHROOM SAUCE

Mushroom sauce will add flavor to any meats or even vegetables. Its richness makes one feel that it is high in calories, but the little cream and whole-wheat flour used are minute and are offset by any calorie–neutralizer salads or vegetables served at the same meal.

Fresh mushrooms, or a can of button mushrooms
3 tablespoons of brandy
3/4 cup real cream or evaporated milk
4 tbsp. butter
1-1/2 cups white wine
juice of 2 lemons
4 tbsp. whole-wheat flour
salt and pepper to taste

Sauté the mushrooms with a little real butter for flavor. As they simmer, add the lemon juice. Lay mushrooms aside, melt a little more butter and stir in flour, making a smooth paste. Cook for only a minute or two, then add the mushrooms, brandy and wine, stirring until it is thick. Now add cream, salt and pepper.

WINE MARINADE

Meats are more flavorful if soaked in a marinade sauce overnight. An excellent wine marinade can be made as follows:

2 cups of red wine (use white wine if preferred)
3 sliced onions
7 black peppercorns
3 cloves garlic

2 bay leaves
Some basil, tarragon, and thyme, mixed together

When the above ingredients are thoroughly mixed together, add the herbs and let stand to absorb taste. Soak meats you wish to marinate in refrigerator overnight. This adds a great taste with no extra calories.

SALAD DRESSING À LA CREME

You can make this delicious dressing by using the creamy-style salad dressings found in powder form in most grocery stores. These are sometimes called ranch dressing.

2 envelopes of creamy dressing powder
1 cup of tomato juice
4 tbs. vinegar

Mix together in a bowl with 4 tbs. of water, shake in a glass jar and store in the refrigerator. It will keep for a long time.

OIL AND CHOPPED GARLIC SALAD DRESSING

This is a fine basic salad dressing that can be made by chopping up three or four cloves of garlic. Put in a glass jar and pour over the garlic about two cupfuls of vegetable oil, or if you prefer for taste, real olive oil. Prepare several jars of this dressing and let them stand for two or three days. This dressing can be poured over salads of lettuce, cucumbers, green peppers, mushrooms, watercress, or spinach leaves. Mix the garlic dressing thoroughly with the vegetables, and then add a few tablespoons of tarragon vinegar and mix before serving. You can also use wine vinegar or apple cider vinegar.

HOLLANDAISE SAUCE

2 tbs. cream
1/2 tsp. salt or salt substitute
4 egg yolks
touch of cayenne pepper
1/2 cup butter or margarine
1/2 tsp. dry mustard

Put the following ingredients in a bowl and set into a pan of hot water. Mix together the egg yolks, vinegar, cream, salt and pepper.

Cook over the moderate heat and beat with an egg beater. Do not boil the water but let it become hot. When these ingredients are beginning to thicken add the margarine or butter, beating it until the butter melts.

This hollandaise sauce is delicious served over broccoli, green beans and asparagus. It is also excellent served over eggs Benedict.

YOUR OWN LOW-CALORIE MAYONNAISE

4 egg yolks	1/2 tsp. white pepper
2 tsp. salt	1/2 cup lemon juice
1/2 tsp. paprika	2-1/2 cups corn oil
2 tsp. dry mustard	

In a bowl combine the lemon juice, egg yolks and seasonings. Stir with a rotary beater while adding salad oil slowly, about 1 tablespoon at a time, until all the oil has been used. Add another tablespoon of lemon juice while adding the balance of the salad oil. Beat until it is thick. Store in refrigerator.

MORE HINTS ON HOW TO GIVE
YOUR TASTE BUDS AN EXTRA BOOST

Many times your reducing diet can be made more tasteful by adding a few ingredients that are found in most kitchens. For instance, you can add soybean sauce with a touch of Worcestershire sauce to pep up your rice, vegetables or other foods, including meats and fish.

When cooking dietetic foods, add a touch of sherry wine to the sauce. (This is not enough to do harm to your diet.)

A very good salad dressing may be made by mixing a little ketchup with mayonnaise and a little apple cider vinegar. A small amount of mayonnaise will not harm you when dieting, for you need some oil each day.

While dieting you should always keep in your refrigerator leftover meats, chicken, hamburger, chicken livers, leg of lamb or other meats. Serve with sauces to make them more appetizing. These can be used for lunches or between-meal snacks.

To keep your hunger-stat happy you can nibble slices of bologna, cheese, yogurt and cold shrimp between meals in small quantities. Dieting should never become boring and monotonous.

CHAPTER 10

The Added Plus
Calorie–Neutralizer Foods
for Greater Joy
in Love and Marriage

You can add years of enjoyment to your love life through the added plus calorie–neutralizer foods. Certain foods give greater sexual stimulus and response than the ordinary, high-carbo-hydrate diet in which most people indulge. These calorie–neutralizer added foods will give you the zest for living and the vitality you need to enjoy romance to the fullest.

This chapter tells about these special foods and shows how you can add them to your diet even while you are losing weight, so you can begin to experience immediate benefits in your romantic relationships.

SCIENTISTS PROVE FOODS AFFECT
EFFICIENCY AND SEXUAL ACTIVITY

A recent study by scientists and nutritionists on the effects of food on physical efficiency and sexual activity determined the following: If a person ate the normal three meals a day he usually overate. Most of the foods lacked nutritive value, making him feel sluggish and affecting his sexual potency. When the person ate smaller meals six times a day, with live, vital foods, such as in the calorie–neutralizer diet, the person gained in vitality, felt less irritable and nervous, and had stronger sexual drives.

The reason for this amazing change, the scientists found, is that the body requires certain amino acids that are to be found mainly in protein foods. By eating only three times a day there was less chance that all the 22 different amino acids would be included in the food intake. When the meals are increased to six a day there is a better chance that most of these important amino acids will be taken into the body.

These rich amino acids are found most frequently in fish, meat, cheese, soybeans and brown rice. They help regulate the system, they keep the sexual energies high but do not add fat calories to the body. As most of the essential amino acids are included in the new calorie–neutralizer reducing diet, and also in the lifetime, normal sustaining diet, you can obtain these valuable elements each day and maintain perfect balance in your diet.

NEW DISCOVERY: LECITHIN KEEPS
SEXUAL VIGOR AT HIGH LEVELS

Lecithin is most important in maintaining the life function of the body cells and in keeping the body's sexual vigor at a high level, even in advanced age.

A diet rich in amino acids and high in daily supplies of lecithin not only furnishes the body with super-energy for daily living, but adds that extra boost to the emotions that makes romance more enjoyable and enduring.

The following foods are high in amino acids and also in lecithin:

all cuts of beef, veal, pork and lamb
soybeans, soybean flour, oil and powder
fish
cheese
beans, navy and lima
lentils
brown rice

Lecithin can be obtained in certain seeds which can be eaten as between-meal snacks, such as sunflower, pumpkin and sesame seeds. These seeds contain more lecithin than soybeans and should be eaten daily to give you greater vitality and energy and to keep sexual vigor at high levels.

65-YEAR-OLD MAN RESTORED TO SEXUAL POTENCY

When I first met Roland T. he seemed like a very tired, old man, although he was only 65 years old. His wife complained that Roland had not been sexually active for three years. He was about 20 pounds overweight but his problem seemed to be something other than this fact.

I put Roland on the new calorie–neutralizer reducing diet and within three weeks time he had easily lost the extra pounds and was his normal weight. However, he still showed no change in his sexual desires.

I recalled the work I had done a few years before in biochemistry, where lecithin had played a significant part in that research. We had used soybean oil, soybean flour and soybean powder in baking breads and cakes. This, coupled with eating pumpkin, sunflower and sesame seeds, all rich in lecithin, had seemed to have a marked effect on people, reviving their interest in sex and giving them greater vigor and vitality.

Roland began this lecithin regimen, eating the seeds between meals, and continued for one month. He reported experiencing a renewed interest in sex and greater feelings of physical enjoyment.

SEXUAL ACTIVITY ALSO STIMULATED BY MINERALS IN THE DIET

Minerals also play a significant role in sexual arousal. Most people suffer from mineral depletion and do not get the required amount in their daily diet. This brings about lowered vitality and causes a person to feel tired and depleted.

An active sex life demands that the body be in a high state of energy and function on a high level of emotion.

OBTAIN IMPORTANT MINERALS
THROUGH CALORIE–NEUTRALIZER FOODS

There are at least 16 minerals that can be obtained from food sources. I shall deal with only 8 of the most important of these, the ones considered essential to human nutrition. Then I list the calorie–neutralizer foods that contain them.

Iron

Iron is essential in the diet because it helps the blood carry oxygen throughout the body. It also helps eliminate carbon dioxide from cells, keeps the bloodstream in good health and gives the body more energy. It is helpful in avoiding anemia. Iron is also needed to send messages from the brain to the entire body. We also need iron in the daily diet to help the body assimilate nutrients to keep the body in perfect health and give it sexual vigor.

You can obtain daily supplies of iron in your diet from the following calorie–neutralizer foods:

liver	dried peaches
whole-wheat products	eggs
apricots	meats
wheat germ	bran
lentils	prunes
barley	blackstrap molasses
yeast	raisins

IRON DEFICIENCY MADE HER CONSTANTLY FATIGUED

Teresa A. was 45 years old and about 15 pounds overweight when she came into the diet workshop to find out why she was constantly fatigued and could hardly get through her household tasks each day. Her family doctor could find nothing wrong with her, although he did find she was slightly anemic. He gave her some medication for this but made no changes in her diet.

Teresa had four children, but they were old enough to take care of themselves. She found that from early morning to late afternoon she simply had to lie down and rest. She awakened each morning more fatigued than when she retired at night.

Teresa confessed to me that she had lost all interest in sex after the birth of her second child. Her husband was still young and virile and desired sex, but for Teresa it became a boring experience that she had to endure.

On the calorie–neutralizer diet Teresa lost her extra 15 pounds in exactly ten days, but her fatigue and other symptoms continued. I then remembered research I had done in my biochemistry studies which showed that a lack of iron in the diet could cause many of the mental and physical symptoms from which Teresa suffered.

I suggested that Teresa check with her doctor to see if she could make changes in her food intake. After he gave his okay, Teresa added liver twice a week to her diet, and more calorie–neutralizer vegetables and fruits that were rich in iron and other valuable minerals. She sprinkled wheat germ on her salads and in her soups, and also took wheat germ oil. She ate two eggs each day and had a milkshake made with skimmed milk and blackstrap molasses, powdered lecithin, brewer's yeast and wheat germ oil. She flavored the milkshake with vanilla and had it twice a day, between meals.

After two weeks Teresa reported that she once again had an interest in sexual relations with her husband. She felt more energetic than ever before. She was thriving on the sustaining diet, which was rich in iron and lecithin, as well as other necessary nutrients.

Calcium

Calcium is needed to build strong teeth and bones. Vitamin D helps the body absorb calcium from the digestive tract and utilize it for skeletal and tooth structure. A calm nervous system also depends on sufficient calcium in the diet. When there is not enough calcium in the diet the body is forced to borrow this important mineral from the bones and this can soon lead to a weakened skeletal system. This is especially important for senior citizens who often have difficulty in walking because of years of calcium deficiency.

Many of the calorie–neutralizer foods given in our daily reducing menus contain large amounts of calcium. These include leafy vegetables, whole grains, egg yolk, skimmed milk, cottage cheese, seafood, buttermilk, blackstrap molasses, most cheeses, whole milk and lemons and oranges, as well as poultry.

Iodine

Iodine is considered important for the normal functioning of the thyroid gland and also to help the body's metabolism. If you become easily fatigued after a little effort and experience a let-down feeling in the middle of the day, it could be because there is a lack of iodine in the diet. A severe case of iodine deficiency can even lead to the formation of a goiter.

You can obtain sufficient iodine from such foods as shrimps, lobsters, oysters, sea greens, many different seafoods and iodized salt.

Copper

Copper works in conjunction with iron to help avoid anemia and enrich the blood. It also plays an important part in pigment formation. When it is lacking in the human diet it can lead to premature gray hair.

Copper can be obtained from leafy greens, oatmeal, soybeans, liver, wheat germ, bran, huckleberries, blackstrap molasses and egg yolk.

Manganese

This important mineral is essential to activate the body's enzymes. It works with phosphorous and calcium to cause normal reproductive functions and increase the maternal instincts in women. If this mineral is lacking in the daily diet there will be an appreciable lessening of the sexual interest and interference with the perfect functioning of the reproductive glands.

Manganese can be found in whole grains, cereals and green vegetables. It is seldom found in refined foods such as white flour or rice, but is in the natural grains, such as wheat and brown rice. Wheat germ is high in this mineral. Sprinkle wheat germ over salads and use it as a breakfast food.

LACK OF MANGANESE AND 55 POUNDS OVERWEIGHT CAUSED PROBLEMS

Wendy H. came into the diet workshop because she was 55 pounds overweight. She was 38 years old, and had two children, ages 8 and 12. Her weight was her main concern. She felt it accounted for her husband's lack of interest in her sexually, and her own lack of interest in her children or her home. Wendy had developed what she called a "lazy attitude" toward everything; she let the house become untidy and the dishes pile up in the sink for three or four meals. Her main interest during the day was in watching soap operas on TV and eating.

What impressed me most in taking Wendy's case history was the fact that she no longer felt affectionate toward her children or husband. This problem had been accelerating for a period of three or four years, during which time she had also gained 55 pounds.

Wendy served meals that seemed to be totally lacking in green vegetables and whole grains. She ate mainly carbohydrates with heavy portions of red-blooded meat. She did not have the energy to prepare green, leafy vegetables or make up tasty salads, so she served mainly meat, potatoes and sometimes canned peas, corn or string beans. Such a diet lacked many of the necessary minerals that the body must have to function properly.

First we worked out a suitable calorie–neutralizer reducing diet for Wendy. We added such green vegetables as spinach, turnip greens, beet tops, and plenty of greens in salads, and this assured her of receiving sufficient amounts of manganese in her diet. She was told to continue the green vegetables long after she had lost her 55 pounds. For breakfasts she began to eat whole-wheat cereals and a slice of whole-wheat toast, with two eggs and coffee. As her compulsive eating habits had to be controlled, she was given a bowl of soup between meals, with many nourishing snacks of low-calorie foods such as shrimp, chicken and liver. She was also permitted to eat as often as she wished, if she stayed with the fruits and vegetables that were in the calorie–neutralizer list. In a period of six weeks Wendy lost the 55 pounds. Her relationships with her husband and children vastly improved.

Sodium

Sodium is an important aid to the absorption of all the other minerals by the body. Many people mistakenly believe that table salt is sodium but it is actually sodium chloride and during dieting it should be avoided. Sodium in its natural form can be obtained in such calorie–neutralizer foods as celery, green string beans, sea kelp and sea salt.

Phosphorous

Phosphorous works like calcium in the body to help bone and tooth formation, and to maintain the skeletal frame in good working order. It is also important in maintaining a high level of fluid content in the brain. Phosphorous reinforces the nerves and muscles and aids the glands in their proper secretions.

Many of the foods given in the calorie–neutralizer diet are rich in phosphorous, including, meats, fish, eggs, cheese, poultry, whole-wheat and soybeans.

Potassium

This important mineral is called nerve food, for it helps the nerves remain healthy and normal. It is essential to the proper functioning of the heart as well as the other muscles of the body. One of its most important functions in the body is as an aid to good digestion and the avoidance of constipation. Potassium is also considered by many scientists as an important aid in preventing insomnia, nervousness and extreme irritability.

Potassium is found abundantly in many of our calorie–neutralizer foods, including green leafy vegetables, carrots, cucumbers, kelp, cranberries, tomatoes, apple cider vinegar, blackstrap molasses, honey and many fruits.

LACK OF POTASSIUM LED TO
CHRONIC CONSTIPATION

Phillip N. came into the diet workshop to lose 20 excess pounds. He later confided that he suffered from chronic constipation that nothing seemed to help.

Phillip complained to his doctor that he suffered from heart palpitations and felt constantly tired, nervous and irritable with his wife and children. At night he took sleeping pills and during the day he took valium to help get through his duties as a bank executive.

Even being 20 pounds overweight could produce unpleasant physical symptoms, so I put Phillip on the usual calorie–neutralizer diet, with plenty of potassium-rich foods such as green leafy vegetables, cucumbers and carrots, blackstrap molasses and honey.

The change in Phillip was amazing. He lost the excess 20 pounds in a little over two weeks. When he reported to his doctor and told him he no longer needed sleeping pills to make him sleep or valium to keep him calm, I knew he was on the right path. Most important of all, Phillip no longer had constipation problems; his system was regular, and he stopped taking medications for the condition. His temperament changed drastically; he became calmer and more efficient in his work. His wife and children found him less volatile and more easy-going than before he began his diet.

EVEN WHEN YOUR WEIGHT IS NORMAL
YOU NEED VITAMINS AND MINERALS

Vitamins and minerals are daily essentials if you wish to keep your body functioning properly. Even when you are back to your normal weight you should include many of the calorie–

neutralizer natural foods that contain the important vitamins and minerals you need.

A healthy sexual appetite depends on maintaining a high level of the right vitamins and minerals through a diet of natural foods. The spark of youth is ignited when you have all of the vital elements present in the daily diet. This depends on the health of the body and the youthful expression of love throughout your adult life.

CHAPTER 11

Delicious Calorie–Neutralizer Recipes to Supplement Your Reducing Diet

Many people need to continue on the calorie–neutralizer diet to lose more than 20 to 30 pounds. If you are in that category you can supplement the menus given in Chapter 4 by using any of the recipes I shall now give.

Add these recipes to the daily reducing menus and alternate any of the meat or fish dishes for some of these more tasty foods.

Despite the fact that some of these recipes appear to be hearty and rich in calories, remember that at each meal you will eat enough of the calorie–neutralizer fruits and vegetables to offset the extra calories in the meal. In this way you will not put on more weight but you will see the pounds continue to melt away.

The following calorie–neutralizer recipes give plenty of foods in the three main categories that are essential to good nutrition even when reducing: proteins, carbohydrates and fats.

There will be new protein meat dishes and recipes for seafoods, which include shrimps, crabs, lobsters and oysters. You can also use some of these vegetable recipes to supplement your calorie–neutralizer menus. If you decide to follow the vegetarian way of life, these recipes for preparing new and interesting vegetable dishes will make it easier for you to diet and help you continue on your normal, sustaining diet for life.

THE FOOD GOURMET WHO LOST 65 POUNDS

When I first met Cynthia L. at the diet workshop, I was impressed by her intense interest in foods of all kinds. Her friends and family considered her quite a gourmet cook, with a wide range of dishes that she had learned at a special cooking class for housewives at a local, community project. She showed the evidences of her taste for rich foods in her round, beaming face, with two double chins, huge bosom and extremely broad hips. When she admitted that she weighed 65 pounds more than her normal 125, I began to see clearly what had happened to her over the years. Cynthia was the victim of overeating rich dishes that were calorie-ridden. She laughingly said, "I doubt if your calorie–neutralizer diet will help me much. I've tried three other reducing systems and none of them worked for me." Cynthia said she could not stay with any reducing plan because she so enjoyed food that she felt constantly starved while dieting.

I then began to work out a special calorie–neutralizer diet that would give Cynthia many of the rich foods she had so enjoyed in the past, but without the carbohydrates and sweets that had wreaked such havoc with her. She prepared special dishes of meat, fish and poultry, such as lobster Newburg, shrimp, crabmeat salads, roasts, stews and omelets. This gave her such a daily variety of dishes that she was constantly on a gourmet's round of taste pleasure without going off her diet.

STEAK AND MUSHROOMS

You may use any cut of steak for this recipe but it should be sliced thin. Filet steak is preferable as it can be cut into thin slices so the sauce may permeate the meat more easily.

2 filet steaks
6 tbs. butter or cooking oil
1 tbs. Worcestershire sauce
4 tbs. brandy
1 tsp. mustard
2 tsp. rosemary
2 cups mushrooms, sliced
salt and pepper to taste

Put the sliced steaks into a pan and fry, adding the rosemary. Cook only a few minutes on each side. After you take steak from the pan put the other ingredients in and boil for a few moments.

The steak can now be served covered with the sauce. You can serve a salad made of calorie–neutralizer vegetables such as lettuce, cucumbers, watercress and peas, with a French dressing.

SAUTÉED LIVER STEAK

Liver is a very important meat that should be eaten at least once a week while reducing. You can prepare it in an unusual way to avoid the dryness that often comes when liver is broiled. Even though this recipe calls for the liver to be fried in butter, these extra calories can be offset by the calorie–neutralizer vegetables served with the dinner.

2 lbs. liver (calf's or beef liver may be used)
1 cup skimmed milk
2 grated onions
3 beaten eggs
1 clove garlic, minced
1 cup whole-wheat flour
1/2 tsp. basil
5 tbs. lemon juice
3 cups cracker crumbs
1/2 cup butter (if preferred, use cooking oil)
salt and pepper to taste

Liver should not be too thickly sliced. Sprinkle first with the lemon juice and then thoroughly saturate the liver with the other mixed dry ingredients such as flour, crumbs and basil. In a separate dish put the eggs, skimmed milk and minced garlic; then place the liver in the mixture. Add more cracker crumbs to the liver. Place in a pan and fry in hot butter. Remember, liver should be cooked for only a few moments. It hardens and becomes rubbery if cooked too long.

With this tasty dish serve two calorie–neutralizer vegetables such as broccoli and squash.

CHICKEN WITH WINE

1 chicken cut into pieces
2 cloves of garlic, crushed
3 sliced stalks of celery
1 large onion, sliced
chopped parsley
1 cup white cooking wine
1/2 cup sour cream
4 carrots, sliced
3 cups of cooked brown rice
pepper and salt to taste

Salt and pepper the chicken, then place it into a casserole dish, with all the ingredients above, except the sour cream and rice. Cover and bake for about 1 hour at 375 degrees. When it is finished, stir in the cream and serve on a bed of cooked brown rice.

No vegetables are needed with this tasty dish, for the brown rice furnishes the calorie–neutralizer that keeps this dish from adding weight. The carrots, onion, celery and garlic also add to the value of the calorie–neutralizers.

BEEF COOKED IN BRANDY SAUCE

2 fillets cut into slices
2 slices ham
2 slices Swiss cheese
4 oz. mushrooms, sautéed in butter
4 oz. cooking oil (butter may be used if preferred)
4 oz. brandy
2 oz. Béarnaise sauce (recipe given in Chapter 9)

Place slices of steak into pan with oil or butter and sauté for a few moments. While still in the pan add the brandy. Now place the Béarnaise sauce with the mushrooms over the steaks. Put pieces of ham on top and leave for a few moments. Melt cheese on top of the steak, ham and mushrooms, and serve hot.

Serve a calorie–neutralizer vegetable with this, such as asparagus or broccoli, with suitable sauce.

SWISS STEAK WITH TOMATO SAUCE

3 lbs. rump steak
1-1/2 cups tomato sauce
large onion chopped up fine
1 cup whole-wheat flour

Mix together the tomato sauce and flour and place the sauce in a pan. Put the steak on top; cover with the chopped onion and whatever sauce remains. Bake in a 375-degree oven for about 1 hour.

Serve a calorie–neutralizer vegetable with this delicious dish, such as beets, string beans or cauliflower. You can also have a green leafy salad with low-calorie dressing before the meal.

CHILI CON CARNE

4 large onions, sliced
2 lbs. ground beef
2-10 oz. cans whole tomatoes
2 tbs. chili powder
1 clove crushed garlic
1 crushed bay leaf
2 cans of kidney beans (without liquid)
3 teaspoons soy sauce

Cook sliced onions in oil; do not overcook. Place ground meat in frying pan alone and cook until brown. Add the chili powder, bay leaf and salt and pepper, and simmer for about 10 minutes. Add the garlic, tomatoes and soy sauce, and cook gently for 5 minutes. Mix in the onions in a casserole dish and cook for about 1 hour at 375 degrees.

Serve a calorie–neutralizer salad of cucumbers, lettuce, tomatoes, green onions and watercress before the meal.

ROAST BEEF WITH MUSHROOM SAUCE

6 lb. cut of beef
2 lbs. mushrooms
4 tbs. butter (or cooking oil)
1/2 cup wheat flour
4 oz. grated cheese
1/2 tsp. mustard
2 pints skimmed milk

6 peppercorns
3 chopped onions
4 cloves crushed garlic
2 crushed bay leaves
2 tbsp. lemon juice
salt and pepper to taste

After roasting the beef, cut it into 1/2-inch slices. Cook the fresh mushrooms in a little oil to soften. (If canned mushrooms are used, use the button variety.) Mix together the peppercorns, onions and bay leaf in the milk, and cook for about 5 minutes. Melt some butter and mix the flour to make a paste. Mix in the sauce made with skimmed milk and stir while it simmers for a few moments. Add the seasoning. Mix the mushrooms into the sauce and add the lemon juice, salt and pepper.

Spread this mixture over the sliced meat and put into a casserole dish prepared for the oven. Beat the cheese into the white sauce, add the mustard, and pour the sauce over the meat, which has already been covered with mushrooms. Sprinkle grated cheese on top and brown for a few moments in oven.

This is a very hearty protein meat dish that should be served with a green salad and one green vegetable, such as peas or asparagus. This dish may also be prepared with roast veal instead of beef.

FOODS LOW IN CALORIES
KEEP A PERSON FROM BEING HUNGRY

People gain weight because they overeat rich foods that only reinforce their hunger. They often skip breakfast, have a light lunch, and then overdo on the rich calories for dinner. Such people often have between-meal snacks to alleviate hunger pangs, and soon put on extra pounds. The following case illustrates this.

SOAP OPERA TV STAR LOST ROLE BECAUSE OF
UNCONTROLLED WEIGHT

Many times on TV soap opera characters are killed off for some reason or other. This happened to one particular young star because she was 25 pounds too heavy and the cameras registered this fact brutally. She was shocked. She no longer fit the description of the character she was playing, which was that of a very smart, sophisticated, fashion plate in high society who attracted one man after another. The producers canceled her contract and conveniently killed her off in the series, leaving the young actress bitter and worried she would never again get a good part.

In taking her case history I found immediately the cause for her gain in weight. She seldom ate any breakfast, taking only two cups of coffee with a piece of toast. By ten in the morning her energy was so low she would eat doughnuts with coffee, or a chocolate bar, thinking this would give her energy. By lunch-time she was half-starved again, and would eat a hamburger on a roll, drink a coke or other sugared soft drink, and many times she would have cake or pie.

This type of eating and between-meal snacking is bound to have serious effects on the body, and soon she gained weight to a point where she no longer photographed well.

When this young actress came to our diet workshop she still looked beautiful and carried the pounds rather well, but keep in mind the fact that the camera makes a person look from 5 to 10 pounds heavier than in real life. For camera purposes she was a good 35 pounds overweight.

During her period of dieting, using the calorie–neutralizer system, she was given a long list of in-between-meal snacks she could eat when she felt hungry. She had a wide variety of foods to eat at each meal and the diet was no great effort for her. At the end of three weeks she had lost the full 25 pounds and she had new publicity photos taken in bathing suits and evening gowns. She was once again the svelte, youthful beauty she had been before. Her agent immediately placed her in another TV series where she went on to become one of the biggest hits of the day! She kept at all times in her dressing room such low-calorie vegetables and fruits as radishes, celery stalks, tomatoes, cucumber slices, cantaloupe, watermelon, apples, cherries, strawberries, oranges and grapefruit. Whenever she felt hungry she ate her fill of these calorie–neutralizer foods. This satisfied her appetite so she did not consume high-calorie foods for lunch or dinner.

RECIPES FOR DELICIOUS SEAFOODS
TO ADD VARIETY TO MEALS

You can use seafoods prepared in different ways to add variety to your calorie–neutralizer menus. Substitute fish often for meat proteins, as it is a better form of protein than meat. You can have seafood for lunch and meat for dinner. If you use the calorie–neutralizer salads and vegetables to prevent absorption of too many calories, you need not worry about the rich sauces that are sometimes suggested with these recipes.

You can begin any evening meal with a delicious oyster soup that will fool guests into thinking you are not really on a reducing diet.

OYSTER SOUP

20 to 25 oysters (serves four people)
4 or 5 cups of chicken consommé
2 cups of dry white wine
salt and pepper to taste

Add the wine to the hot consommé. Before it boils add oysters and seasoning. Remove the oysters in a few moments so they are not overcooked. Serve with a calorie–neutralizer salad or two vegetables.

CRAB AND TOMATO SOUP

fresh crab meat, if possible (canned crab meat can also be used)
3 onions, chopped
4 tablespoons of butter
2 cups of tomato purée
4 cups milk
4 tablespoons sherry
1-1/2 pounds fresh peas (canned will do if not available fresh)

Cook together the onions and peas in butter, with a little water. When cooked slightly put into a blender and mix with the milk. Warm tomato purée and keep in a separate dish. Flake the crab meat and cook in butter for only a few moments. Add the sherry wine and flavor to taste with salt and pepper. The same type of soup may be made with shrimps cut up, or with lobster or lobster tails.

Serve this hearty soup with two calorie–neutralizer vegetables or a green salad of cucumbers, lettuce, tomatoes and radishes. It makes a hearty lunch or can be served as the first course of any dinner.

Crab meat is always a very hearty seafood to add to your reducing menus, for it has few fat calories. The following recipe makes a very tasty lunch or dinner dish when served with a calorie–neutralizer green salad.

CRAB MEAT WITH MUSHROOMS

(Use fresh crab meat when available; if not, use canned or frozen.)
1 lb. crab meat
2 tsp. lemon juice
4 tbs. scallions, chopped fine
3 tbs. butter
24 large mushrooms

Sauté the scallions in butter until they are soft. Mix in the crab meat and cook a few moments. Make a cream sauce into which you mix the crab meat with the lemon juice. Cut the stems off the big mushrooms and fill them with the crab meat; then bake in the oven at 350 degrees until the mushrooms are cooked slightly. Do not cook for more than 10 to 12 minutes.

CRAB MEAT AND AVOCADO SALAD

Avocados are high in oil content and are suggested only when you use calorie–neutralizer vegetables or fruits to counteract the fat calories. Occasionally you can make up a crab meat and avocado salad as a main luncheon or dinner course if no other fat calories are served. This is a hearty salad and requires no meat course or soup with it, but you can serve a green leaf salad if you wish.

1 large can of cooked or fresh crab meat (cook it slightly)
2 tbs. low-calorie mayonnaise
4 scallions, chopped
2 tsp. vegetable oil (olive oil may be used but it is high in fat calories)
2 avocados
paprika

Mix the crab meat with cut-up avocado. Add mayonnaise, oil and paprika for color. Serve in a glass dish.

SHRIMP, CRAB MEAT AND GREEN PEPPERS, STUFFED

The green peppers are on the calorie–neutralizer list and make a fine background for this delicious crab-meat main dish.

as many large green peppers as needed
1 lb. of fresh or canned crab meat (or use shrimp)
1-1/2 cups cream sauce
Parmesan cheese
paprika

Prepare the green peppers by cutting off the tops and taking out the seeds. Boil for about 5 minutes; do not overboil. Add the crab meat or shrimp to the cream sauce; season with salt, pepper and a little paprika. Fill the peppers and sprinkle with Parmesan cheese. Cook in a moderate oven for about 30 minutes.

DELICIOUS CREAM SAUCE FOR
LOBSTER, SHRIMP OR CRAB-MEAT DISHES

Many delicious fish dishes can be served with this cream sauce that is rich in calories. However, as some oil is needed even when reducing, you can use low-calorie mayonnaise, real cream or sour cream. Remember, when you use such calorie-rich sauces for any recipe, you can always eat a calorie–neutralizer salad with the meal, or serve two of the calorie–neutralizer vegetables on the no. 1 priority list.

1 cup of sour cream or real cream
1-1/2 cups of vegetable oil
1/2 cup dry white wine
1 tbs. tarragon vinegar

Put into blender and mix together. Serve this sauce for cold salad dishes made with crab meat, shrimp or lobster, or you can serve it hot.

Before continuing with other delicious recipes to supplement the calorie–neutralizer reducing diet, let me assure you that you will never feel deprived of tasty, nourishing dishes while losing weight. As you see by these and other recipes, gourmet-style cooking and eating is still possible while you lose excess weight.

SOUTHERN COOKING STARTED HER
ON WEIGHT GAIN OF 35 POUNDS

Loretta D. told me in our first interview that her weight had always been between 125 and 130 pounds. She was a school teacher and during summer vacation she visited relatives in Alabama for two months. She was on a constant round of cocktail parties and dinners at the homes of friends and relatives. She enjoyed the good old southern cooking she had known as a child: fried chicken, sweet potatoes, corn bread dripping with fresh country butter and pecan pie for dessert. Vegetables were always drenched in some rich, cream sauce that made them delicious but fattening. At the end of the third week of vacation she began letting out the waists of her dresses. She checked the bathroom scales in alarm to find she had gained 15 pounds!

Loretta decided to stop gorging on the rich southern cooking, but how can you refuse an aunt who has been in the kitchen all day preparing the feast spread before you? When the desserts came (not one but two), she couldn't insult her hostess by not eating them and exclaiming about their genuinely delicious goodness. But the results soon showed in continued weight gain. By the end of her summer vacation, when she returned to her work up north, Loretta tipped the scales at 160 pounds, which did not look well on her five foot four frame. The worst result from overeating of rich foods was that Loretta craved the carbohydrates and sweets she had grown accustomed to eating down south.

Loretta told me in her first interview that she had waited this long before seeking help because she could not face the prospect of a strict diet of "cottage cheese and lettuce." When she learned of the varied bill of fare with the calorie–neutralizer foods, she began to substitute such rich dishes as beef in wine sauce, steak and mushrooms, crab meat with mushrooms, baked fish à la Parmesan, chicken with wine, and other savory dishes for the more prosaic ones on the calorie–neutralizer diet, and she was able to enjoy dieting for the first time in her life.

In two weeks Loretta lost 22 pounds. Then it was simple for

her to continue on the extension menus until she was once again back to her normal 125 pounds.

DIETING SHOULD BE A FUN EXPERIENCE

Continue with these supplemental recipes and add them to your calorie–neutralizer menus. Make dieting a fun experience while you eat rich, gourmet-type foods.

SCALLOPS IN WHITE WINE

This is a delicious dish, low in calories, and may be served with a crisp green salad, using calorie–neutralizer vegetables.

20 or more scallops
2 cups white wine
3 tbs. butter
2 cups dietetic bread crumbs
salt and pepper to taste

Cook the scallops for about 4 minutes in butter. Add the wine, salt and pepper and cook slowly for about 2 minutes more. Put the bread crumbs into a dish with melted butter and when the scallops are cooked, serve them on top of the bread crumbs.

LOBSTER À LA NEWBURG

You can use anywhere from 2 to 4 lobsters for this tasty, popular dish. Take the meat and cut it up into small pieces. Blend together 4 egg yolks, 2 cups of cream and 2 tbs. flour. Stir until thick. In the meantime, let the lobsters simmer in melted butter. Add about 1 cup of sherry wine to the eggs, cream, flour and butter, and when thoroughly cooked, pour over the lobsters and serve on pieces of whole-wheat toast.

This dish is high in calories so be sure that you serve either two calorie–neutralizer vegetables or a crisp green salad.

BAKED FILLET OF SOLE STUFFED WITH SHRIMP

Fillet of sole or any fresh fish may be used for this dish, boned and in whole strips. You also need about 12 or 13 shrimp. Cook the shrimp for only a few moments in water that has half a sliced onion, bay leaf, salt and pepper. Remove water and save it for later use as sauce in which to bake the fish.

Grind the shrimp fine, put in two beaten eggs, 1 tbs. flour, a little white wine and 2 tbs. cream. Stir all together. If stuffing fillet of sole, place one fish on dish, put the stuffing on top of it and lay another fish on top in a casserole dish until you have used all the fish. Then add a little of the broth you saved, and cook for about 20 minutes in a moderately hot oven. Parmesan cheese may be sprinkled on top before serving.

CREAMED FILLET OF SOLE AND MUSHROOMS

This fish dish is quick to prepare and makes a tasty luncheon dish served with a calorie–neutralizer green salad.

as many fillets of fish as you wish to serve
a can of cream of mushroom soup
bread crumbs and grated cheese

Cook fish in water until tender, then remove bones and cut into small pieces. Put these into mushroom soup, and place in a casserole dish. Sprinkle bread crumbs and grated cheese on top and bake in a moderate oven until brown.

CHICKEN SALAD WITH LOBSTER

3 or 4 chicken breasts, cooked
about 1-1/2 lbs. lobster meat, cooked
1/2 cup celery, chopped
4 hard-boiled eggs
3 cups shredded lettuce
low-calorie mayonnaise

Mix together cut-up pieces of lobster and chicken. Let stand in a French dressing with chopped-up egg whites and celery for about half an hour. Mix chopped-up egg yolks with mayonnaise, pepper and salt and a little parsley. Serve the chicken and lobster on plates with cut-up lettuce and dressing.

BAKED FISH À LA PARMESAN

as many fish as you wish, preferably fillet of sole
about 6 bacon strips
a little cooking oil

bread crumbs
Parmesan cheese
white wine
salt and pepper to taste

Bone the fish. After rubbing it with cooking oil, place it in bread crumbs and Parmesan cheese mixture. Now add the strips of bacon on top of fish in a casserole dish, put some white wine on it and bake until tender. Serve with sauce or more cheese.

RECIPES TO PREPARE CALORIE–NEUTRALIZER VEGETABLES

ARTICHOKES AND SHRIMP WITH CHEDDAR CHEESE

The artichoke is a marvelous calorie–neutralizer vegetable. Its sturdy structure makes it high in fiber content, in resisting digestion and absorption and in helping to neutralize the Cheddar cheese, cream of mushroom soup and other high calories in a meal. You can serve a salad of calorie–neutralizer raw vegetables with this dish and it becomes a very filling, satisfying meal for dinner.

use two packages of frozen artichoke hearts or prepare fresh
2 small cans of cream of mushroom soup
1 lb or more of fresh shrimp (cut up into small pieces after they are cooked)
salt and pepper to taste

After cooking the artichoke hearts, add the mushroom soup, chopped-up shrimp, and cook for a few minutes on low flame. Add some fresh Cheddar cheese on top of dish when serving. You can also use crab meat or lobster meat instead of shrimp.

ASPARAGUS WITH CREAM SAUCE

Asparagus also falls into the category of fiber-rich, calorie–neutralizer vegetables, as it adds few calories and furnishes enough delaying action in digestion to make calorie absorption difficult. You can make your own cream sauce, based on the recipe given in Chapter 9, or you may use one can of cream of mushroom soup if you choose. Cook the asparagus until the stalks are tender. Combine the mushroom soup in a pan with 2 beaten eggs, a little salt and pepper and a touch of lemon juice. Serve on slices of whole-wheat toast. This makes a delicious luncheon dish if served with a hamburger patty and a small salad.

ASPARAGUS AND MUSHROOM CASSEROLE

This makes a rich and tasty dish for luncheon or dinner. You can make a thick, creamy sauce with golden cream of mushroom soup. Also cut up 6 to 8 large fresh mushrooms. Cook asparagus until tender. Place in the bottom of the casserole dish, add 2 eggs, beaten, to the mushroom soup, cut up Cheddar cheese and put on top. It needs only a little salt, for the cheese furnishes this. Sprinkle on top the sliced fresh mushrooms and bake a few moments until mushrooms are tender. Serve on a bed of brown rice or with a lean meat dish such as beef, lamb or chicken.

BOSTON BAKED BEANS SUBSTITUTE FOR MEAT PROTEIN

The sturdy, fiber-rich navy bean has long been a staple in the American diet. You need not deny yourself this choice food while dieting. You can serve it with any two calorie–neutralizer vegetables, as a side order with a meat dish, or you may have baked beans and brown rice for a sturdy, nourishing protein meal. The combination of the rice and beans neutralizes the carbohydrate nature of both grains and makes them more protein than starch.

Most packages of beans you buy have a recipe printed on the package for baked beans. Here is a recipe that you may use also.

BAKED BEANS

4 cups of white navy beans
1-1/2 tsp. salt
1-1/2 tsp. dry mustard
1 cup of molasses (use part brown sugar and part molasses if you wish)
2 large onions, chopped up fine

Salt pork may be added if you wish but it is better to leave it out while dieting, as it adds many fat calories.

Let the beans stand overnight in water. Boil the next day for about 1 hour until tender. Mix together all the ingredients above, add chopped onion and pour liquid over beans in big crock. Save some of the liquid from the boiled beans to add to the beans while cooking in an oven heated to about 350 degrees. Let cook for several hours. Keep adding the bean liquid when needed to keep the beans moist.

Beans may be served with a crisp calorie–neutralizer salad, for main meal at dinner, or for lunch with frankfurters cut up in beans.

If you want a more pungent taste to the baked beans, add a cup of chili sauce or ketchup to the mixture.

LIMA BEANS À LA GRECO

Lima beans are carbohydrate in nature, but they are also wonderfully alkaline. You can add this tasty member of the bean family to your reducing menus occasionally.

Cooked Greek style the lima beans have a good taste and make a full meal for lunch or dinner.

1 large envelope of lima beans (use the small lima beans rather than the large ones)
2 large onions, sliced
1 small can tomato paste
1 cup of olive oil or cooking oil
salt to taste

Boil the lima beans in enough water to cover them, until the skin is easily removed. Do not add any ingredients while boiling them as this tends to keep the beans from cooking easily.

After about 45 minutes of boiling, add 2 tablespoons of tomato paste, chopped onion, and a cup of olive oil to the boiling beans. Let them continue to boil until the beans are thoroughly cooked. This is usually about 45 minutes to 1 hour.

This delicious dish tends to bring about an alkaline reaction in the digestive processes. If you serve a small salad with the beans you will avoid absorbing the carbohydrates.

Spinach furnishes two basic requirements of the calorie–neutralizer vegetables: It furnishes fiber and bulk with its minerals and elements that are important to nutrition, and it helps neutralize the calories of any rice protein or carbohydrate meal. You can eat spinach by steaming it and adding margarine for flavor, or you can eat it cold as a salad with a delicious low-calorie dressing. You can also cook it and serve it in more tasty forms, as the following two recipes show.

SPINACH AND SOUR CREAM

1 lb. of fresh spinach, steamed until soft
10 mushrooms, fresh or canned
1-1/2 cups sour cream
1 cup Cheddar cheese, chopped
salt and pepper to taste

After cooking the spinach spread it in an oven-proof dish. Arrange the mushrooms over the spinach and bake in the oven for about ten minutes. Before serving it spread sour cream and grated Cheddar cheese on top.

CREAMED SPINACH

2 lbs. of fresh spinach (or frozen)
2-1/2 cups of milk
1 small can cream of mushroom soup
3 eggs, beaten

Steam the spinach until soft, then mix together the milk and eggs. Add the cream of mushroom soup and mix thoroughly. Heat the oven to about 375 degrees and cook until done, about 20 minutes.

You need not serve any other calorie–neutralizer vegetables with the two above recipes. The spinach itself helps neutralize the calories contained in the rich sauces used. If you are serving a beef, fish or steak dinner however, you can add a calorie–neutralizer salad of lettuce, cucumbers and tomatoes to the meal.

Both zucchini and squash are high on the list of added vegetables to the top priority no. 1 list of calorie–neutralizers. They can be prepared in tasty dishes that will add appeal and help fortify against rich calories from other foods served at the same meal.

ZUCCHINI DELIGHT

10 medium-sized zucchini, unpared and sliced
1 large can whole tomatoes, chopped fine
2 large onions, sliced thin
3 large chopped green peppers
2 cups of Italian bread crumbs
1/4 pound Cheddar cheese, sliced

A small chunk of margarine may be spread over the top before baking. Place in a casserole dish alternating layers of zucchini, green pepper, onions and tomatoes. Place Cheddar cheese slices on top. Spread bread crumbs over top and bake covered in moderate oven for about 35 minutes. Test to see when tender and serve hot.

ZUCCHINI À LA ROMA

8 or 10 medium-sized zucchini
4 eggs, beaten
touch of garlic salt
1/4 tsp. black pepper
2 cups evaporated milk
4 tbs. margarine
salt to taste

Cook zucchini slices slightly until nearly done. (Steaming is better than boiling.) Combine margarine, eggs, seasoning and milk in a pan and mix thoroughly. Then pour over the zucchini and bake in a 350-degree oven for about 25 minutes. Do not overcook.

This recipe makes a delicious luncheon dish on a cold day, or it can be used for dinner with any meat, chicken or fish order. Serve with a calorie–neutralizer green salad with low-calorie dressing.

There are several varieties of squash, including summer squash, banana squash, acorn and turban squash, as well as the sturdy winter squash. The following recipe for banana squash gives a tasty side dish for any meal.

BANANA SQUASH WITH SOUR CREAM

Cut up several portions of banana squash into serving sizes. Put into an oven-proof dish with 1 cup of water and bake for about 25 minutes in a 350-degree oven. Mix together sour cream, a touch of paprika, 1/2 cup margarine and 1/4 cup brown sugar. Spread this mixture over squash and bake for a few moments more until tender.

DELICIOUS ACORN SQUASH, GLAZED

Use about 4 acorn squash, cut in half, with seeds removed. Bake in a moderate oven until tender. Prepare small onions, chopped walnuts, 5 tbs. margarine, 4 tbs. brown sugar, salt and cinnamon. Spread mixture over squash and bake for about 15 minutes more. Baste with sauce occasionally.

CHAPTER 12

The Calorie–Neutralizer Sustaining Diet to Remain Slender for Life

The one haunting fear that all dieters have in common is that, after spending agonizing weeks losing weight, they will go right back to the old eating habits that made them fat in the first place.

Most of us are used to eating excessive amounts of carbohydrates over a period of many years. We enjoy the tasty thrill of fattening foods. The carbohydrate habit is difficult to break; it is easy to fall into the habit of eating the wrong foods.

NOW YOU HAVE BROKEN THE CARBOHYDRATE HABIT FOR GOOD

If you have followed the calorie–neutralizer menus for reducing, it can safely be assumed that you have broken the vicious carbohydrate habit for life. Now you are free of the necessity for loading your system with these poisons that clutter up the body's metabolism and which are quickly converted into fat. The body normally stores such fat for future use. This is based on nature's habit over the centuries to store fat on the body during plentiful times so it would be available as energy during lean times. Your body metabolism is still geared to this primitive system of storing foods on the body. We see this same system at work in the camel, who is able to store extra water in its two humps to carry it many miles over a hot, dusty desert without water.

Now, let us assume that you have lost from 10 to 50 pounds of superfluous weight. What system of dieting should you follow for the rest of your life to avoid ever again being overweight?

Such a lifelong plan should include foods that give your body the essential nutrients and vitamins and the daily requirements of proteins, fats and carbohydrates. The normal calorie–neutralizer sustaining diet will furnish you with nourishing foods each day. You will cut out the fat-calorie foods and replace them with the low-calorie foods. You will keep the carbohydrate intake to a minimum. You need about 60 grams of carbohydrate a day; most people consume from 250 to 450 grams a day! As these excess carbohydrates are quickly turned into fat you can see why you will quickly put on weight again if you return to your old habits of eating.

Another reason why you must withdraw from a high-fat, high-calorie diet the rest of your life: Scientists have recently confirmed that a high carbohydrate diet will eventually lead to excessive cholesterol in the blood. This increases your chances for high blood pressure, heart attacks and many other diseases.

SATISFY YOUR SWEET TOOTH DEMANDS WITH LOW-CALORIE FRUITS

When you have an urge to eat pastries, pies, cakes, cookies, ice cream and other rich carbohydrates, you can satisfy this craving by eating all you want of the calorie–neutralizer fruits in lists no. 1 and 2. Your hunger-stat will scream for carbohydrates when you go on this or any diet to lose weight. This is the fat on your body that wants to remain with you, for no fat cells like to be killed off. It must be a gradual weaning process in which you substitute other foods for the fattening ones.

After you have lost the desired number of pounds and go on the lifetime, sustaining calorie–neutralizer diet, there is always the possibility that you might once again revert to the old carbohydrate habits and regain the unwanted pounds. The following case illustrates how this can happen.

DIANA C. REGAINED 20 POUNDS
BY REVERTING TO CARBOHYDRATE HABIT

When Diana C. came into the diet workshop she was 20 pounds overweight from a recently-formed carbohydrate habit. As she watched soap operas while doing her work, she felt the emotions of the characters deeply. Sometimes to assuage her grief over some very touching scene, she would eat a big dish of ice cream, which she kept stocked in her refrigerator for such occasions. This gave her an emotional pick-up and she would be in fine condition until late afternoon, when she felt the urge to have something sweet again. Then it would be cake, cookies or candy, until she felt fully satisfied. She seldom ate much dinner, and when her husband noted she was getting fat around the stomach and hips, he remarked, "I can't understand it. You hardly touch your food and yet you're gaining weight."

When Diana sought help in our diet workshop, she confessed to carbohydrate overeating. I suggested she substitute the calorie–neutralizer fruits for the heavy carbohydrates she was eating.

In exactly three weeks Diana had lost her 20 pounds and once again felt comfortable at 125 pounds. Her husband was delighted and Diana confessed she felt better than ever.

But when she went on the sustaining calorie–neutralizer diet Diana once again strayed into the harmful carbohydrate habit. Instead of sticking with the wide variety of foods she could eat, she began to indulge her sweet tooth, thinking that it would not do any harm. She drank as many as four bottles of soda at a time, each loaded with six spoonfuls of sugar to each bottle! She still ate cookies and candies while watching TV, but she felt that this would do no harm now that her weight was gone.

Within one month Diana had regained most of her former 20 pounds and came back to the diet workshop to find out what she was doing wrong.

By giving Diana more sweet fruits and desserts that were in the calorie–neutralizer lists, she soon overcame the feeling of deprivation and was able to adjust to the new diet quickly. She still ate between meals and while watching TV, but now she substituted the low-calorie fruits and vegetables, like tomatoes, radishes, celery, green peppers and cucumbers. She nibbled on dates, figs and nuts. Even though these are carbohydrates, they are natural sugars and their high calories are offset by fruits and vegetables eaten at regular meals.

Soon Diana was back at her normal weight and felt that she had now broken her carbohydrate habit enough to stay on the sustaining diet the rest of her life.

Many of the foods in the lifetime sustaining diet are given in the calorie–neutralizer diet for losing weight. In addition, I shall give other foods that furnish more low-fat calories in your diet and provide good nutrition.

INCLUDE LOW-FAT SOUPS AS
FUTURE APPETITE KILLERS

An excellent way of killing the appetite so you keep from overeating is to add soups to your daily menus. You can prepare delicious soups, low in fat content, by using the calorie–neutralizer vegetables and lean meats. Cabbage, tomatoes, green peppers, celery, onions and carrots, with boiled meat, all take more energy to digest than they give to your body. Be sure to skim off any fats that might come from the meat you use.

Chicken soup is always a welcome addition to any meal, for it furnishes you with soup and meat at the same time. It is also easy to prepare. Skin the chicken first, as this will help remove the fat. If you do not, let the soup stand in the refrigerator for a while and then skim the fat off the top. You can use celery, carrots and onions to make the soup and boil it for about one hour. This soup is nourishing, low-fat, and will give protein energy. It can be kept stored in the refrigerator for several days, giving you many meals.

Stock up on several ready-mix soups. You can have cream of tomato soup one day, asparagus soup another, as well as cream of chicken, veal, beef, minestrone and vegetable. Served with a delicious salad for lunch or dinner, such soups are great appetite killers and nonfattening.

You can also use a wide variety of legumes for soups, such as lentils, navy beans, peas and lima beans. Lentils can be cooked as a main dish by adding beef frankfurters, which are very filling and nonfattening. Boil the lentils, with one big chopped onion, artificial salt, corn oil, and a touch of tomato paste, to make an appetizing dish. Cut up several beef frankfurters after it is finished and boil for a few more minutes. Serve with a green salad for a luncheon dish. With this you can serve a low-calorie gelatin dessert or a calorie–neutralizer fruit dish.

BETWEEN-MEAL SNACKS SHOULD
BE ENCOURAGED ON SUSTAINING DIET

To avoid being constantly hungry, which often happens when a person loses weight rapidly, it might be wise to indulge your appetite between meals with low-calorie foods. These can include celery, lettuce, tomatoes, cucumbers, green peppers and radishes. Eat as many as you wish until your appetite is satisfied.

You can also snack on tuna, chicken salad or two beef frankfurters. There are low-calorie cheeses which you can also allow yourself, but don't overeat or the calories will begin to add up quickly.

Many people gain weight because they are compulsive eaters; you may recognize this fault in yourself. Make it a point, when you have the strong compulsion to eat big meals, to eat some of the calorie–neutralizer fruits or vegetables, or a shrimp or lobster salad. You can eat all the cantaloupe and watermelon you want until satisfied. Most of the fruits in the calorie–

neutralizer lists take more calories to digest than they give your body, so you can eat up to 4 pounds of vegetables and fruits a day and never gain an ounce!

THE SIX-MEAL DIET THAT CURED
A COMPULSIVE EATER

Henry R. came to the diet workshop after his weight had increased from 175 to 225 pounds in one year. He told me that this would not have bothered him until his doctor found he had very high blood pressure, traces of diabetes and symptoms of heart trouble. As Henry was only 50 years old, these findings alarmed him and he sought help.

Henry had tried to reduce but he felt compelled to eat several times a day. When he named the rich, high-calorie foods he consumed in a day I could see why his weight had shot up in such a short time.

In putting Henry on the calorie–neutralizer diet I realized that I could not cut his calorie intake to 1000 or so a day, for that was what discouraged him quickly with other diets he had tried. I began his diet by permitting him to eat at least six meals a day and as many of the calorie–neutralizer foods as he wished. I eliminated all carbohydrates from his diet for the first two weeks, until I felt he was over that bad habit. Then I slowly added some sweets in the form of desserts to satisfy his hunger-stat.

A typical day's food intake went like this: For breakfast he was permitted a heavy meal, such as bacon and eggs or a mush-room and cheese or onion omelet, with one piece of whole-wheat toast, some butter and marmalade. Some mornings he had eggs Benedict, with whole-wheat toasted English muffins topped with two slices of Canadian bacon and a nonfattening sauce. He had his usual cup of coffee, with real cream but artificial sugar. Henry did not have to wait until lunch time for more food. About 10 A.M. he would eat calorie–neutralizer veg-etables, such as celery, cucumbers, radishes, green peppers and tomatoes . . . all he wanted until his appetite was satisfied. These did not add any calories.

If he got hungry again before lunch, which he usually did,

he would eat leftover meats from dinner or a portion of chicken salad, two frankfurters or six large shrimps. Again he could have calorie–neutralizer vegetables or fruits to reduce the calorie intake. Even though Henry ate more than 2000 calories a day, he continued to lose weight because he ate foods that were not carbohydrates or fattening.

By eating at least six meals a day Henry never felt he was on a diet, and this was psychologically good for him. He lost his 50 pounds in a period of only six weeks without once suffering from hunger pangs, as he had on former diets.

When Henry was back to his normal weight he once again checked with his doctor and found that his blood pressure was normal and his heart condition vastly improved. The blood sugar which was thought due to diabetes returned to normal. His doctor said undoubtedly the loss of weight had led to his complete recovery.

After losing his 50 pounds Henry was put on the lifetime, sustaining calorie–neutralizer diet. This gave him plenty of foods, including between-meal snacks, which kept him full. The foods he ate were all in the calorie–neutralizer lists of nonfattening, low-calorie ones, so he never regained the excess weight and his health was better than ever.

INDULGE YOUR TASTE
FOR MEAT PROTEINS WHILE
ON THIS SUSTAINING DIET

Unless you are a strict vegetarian, you can indulge your taste for meat at least once a day while on this lifetime sustaining diet. Meat is a most desirable form of protein to maintain the body at a high level of energy, without fearing that you will put on excess weight. Only meat contains all the essential amino acids the body requires to maintain good health and a balanced nutrition. Too much meat, if eaten with the wrong combination of fat-calorie vegetables, can make you gain weight. However, a good steak, a patty of ground meat or a slice of roast beef, when eaten with the various vegetables given, will furnish your body with sufficient calories to meet each day's activities, without adding an ounce of excess weight.

Moderate exercise is also useful in maintaining normal body weight. This can be jogging or simple walking, if past the age of 50, swimming, golf, tennis or any sport that you enjoy. If past 50 or 60, however, exercise should be moderate so as not to put too great a strain on the heart.

To avoid absorbing too many fat calories from the meat you should use mostly lean cuts that are nearly fat-free. Unfortunately, even lean meats contain many veins of fat that are not visible on the surface. Select those meats that appear lean and have your butcher trim away all excess fat.

The best way to avoid taking on extra calories is to broil the meat, not fry it. By frying you absorb all the fats that come from the meat. Broiling lets the fat fall into the drip pan and keeps the fat from coating the meat with extra calories.

If you like the taste of fried meat it should be cooked in a nonstick pan that makes it unnecessary to use grease for frying.

AVOID HIGH CHOLESTEROL MEATS

High cholesterol meats such as pork chops, roast loin of pork, bacon and ham or sausages should be eaten sparingly, for they are all high in fat content. However, you need not deny yourself these tasty meats entirely. When you serve them be sure you also eat a big calorie–neutralizer salad, with low-calorie dressing, and at least two of the higher-fiber, calorie–neutralizer vegetables given in the high priority list. This will ensure you of ridding the body of extra fat calories.

Liver is an excellent form of protein, as well as a good source of iron and other valuable elements. Add liver to your sustaining diet at least once a week. Beef liver is actually as nutritious as calf's liver and is not as expensive. It is best to broil the liver, to avoid overcooking it.

ADD SPICES AND HERBS TO MEATS TO MAKE THEM FLAVORFUL

French chefs are experts in adding herbs and spices in the preparation of meat dishes to make them more flavorful. You can prepare your meat dishes with herbs and spices such as basil, garlic, oregano, thyme and bay leaves. Many famous Greek and Italian dishes are prepared with spices, which add to the flavor of most meat dishes.

You can also garnish your meat dishes with various types of fruits, such as sliced pineapple, purple plums, peach halves, prunes and broiled bananas. If you use canned fruits use the type with artificial sugar, or wash the heavy syrup out of the fruits before using them.

You can also add variety to your meat dishes by using ketchup, chili sauce, chili powder, chutney sauce, canned tomatoes, tomato paste, applesauce, mint jelly, cranberry sauce and various relishes.

THE IMPORTANCE OF POULTRY

As there are limited varieties of meats you can use in your sustaining diet, it is wise to include poultry at least once a week. You can use chicken, turkey, squab or guinea hen, all prepared without the usual stuffing. Bake these poultry dishes rather than fry them and avoid eating the fatty skin. Duck and goose should seldom be eaten because of the extra fat calories they contain.

If you wish to add sandwiches to your luncheons, you can use chicken or turkey, with a low-calorie mayonnaise or some other dressing. Be sure to use protein or whole-wheat breads for these sandwiches and avoid white bread, which is usually more fattening. An excellent luncheon can be prepared using chicken or turkey in a sandwich, served with a green salad of calorie–neutralizer vegetables, a low-calorie dressing and a glass of whole milk, coffee or tea. You can also on occasion include low-calorie mayonnaise with your sandwich.

TRY SUBSTITUTING FISH PROTEINS FOR MEAT DISHES

Fish is really a better form of protein than meat. Fish also contains fewer fat calories than most meats. However, if you fry the fish it will add many calories so it is best to broil or bake fish.

Scallops, haddock, flounder, perch and sturgeon furnish

excellent proteins with very little fat. You can also eat small portions of brook trout, porgy and cod, but they are a little higher in fat calories. Use a calorie–neutralizer salad and two vegetables from the no. 1 priority list when you have foods that are high in fat calories.

Crabs, lobsters, shrimps and scallops are low in fat calories. Oysters may also be included in your fish dishes but they should not be fried. Eat them raw or in an oyster stew made with skimmed milk and a little butter, salt and pepper for flavoring.

You can also include tuna fish, canned or fresh, for it is low in fat calories. Tuna packed in ordinary water is best; it may be prepared in a salad or made into sandwiches by adding a little chopped onion and a low-calorie mayonnaise. Sardines are most often packed in oil but you can add them to your sustaining diet if you eat a calorie–neutralizer vegetable or salad with the meal.

There is such a wide variety of fish dishes that can be prepared and used as substitutes for meat, that it might be wise to intersperse these in any future sustaining diet you plan. Where meat dishes are listed in the menus, you can safely substitute a fish dish and still continue to lose weight easily. The following example illustrates how this can be done.

AVERSION TO RED-BLOODED MEAT LED TO ALTERNATIVE FOODS

Louise A. steadily gained weight on a heavy carbohydrate and meat diet; she sought help when the scales showed she was 22 pounds overweight. She told me in her first interview that she did not like red-blooded meat, but ate it because she had always had it at home when she was young. Potatoes, white bread, gravy and rich desserts completed her usual bill of fare, and she had not changed her diet habit over the years.

When she went on the calorie–neutralizer diet to lose her excess pounds Louise asked if she could substitute other foods for meat. I said she could substitute fish or chicken protein instead of other meats. Each day she ate some fish and chicken, with the calorie–neutralizer fruits and vegetables. Between-meal snacks were included, using crab-meat salad, shrimp, lobster and scallops. She began to lose weight after only two days and was able to lose 7 pounds the first week. The second week she lost 10 pounds, and in a short time, she shed the other 5 pounds. She admitted when she went on the lifetime, sustaining diet, that it had been much easier to lose weight than she had dared hope. I told her that on the sustaining diet she could eliminate red-blooded meat entirely and subsist on fish and chicken proteins, with whole milk, grains, vegetables and fruits, without ever gaining weight again or suffering nutritional imbalance.

THE VALUE OF EGG PROTEINS

Eggs are a valuable form of protein and should be included in the lifetime sustaining diet. However, what scientists have discovered about the heavy cholesterol content of eggs should not be ignored. Cholesterol is harmful to the health, so use eggs only two or three times a week, boiled or poached, to avoid cooking them in fats. You can also fry them in a nonsticking pan without using oil. Most of the cholesterol is found in the egg yolk, not the white. Do not try to replace meat protein with egg protein.

MILK PRODUCTS HELP ENRICH
YOUR SUSTAINING DIET WITH PROTEINS

Many nutritionists argue that people do not need milk after they have reached maturity and their teeth and bones are fully formed. The latest scientific research shows that milk is a good source of protein and they suggest that everyone should have at least two glasses of milk a day. Whole milk does contain butter fat. Since this is a form of cholesterol, you might prefer to use skimmed milk fortified with two teaspoonfuls of dried, powdered milk to make it more palatable. If whole milk is used, fortified with vitamins A and D, then reduce your fat intake in such foods as meat and butter. Use margarine as a butter substitute if you fear taking too much cholesterol.

Buttermilk and yogurt are also good for obtaining extra proteins. These can be added to the sustaining diet and taken each day for their high calcium and protein content.

EAT CHEESE PRODUCTS SPARINGLY IN YOUR SUSTAINING DIET

You can eat cottage cheese or pot cheese when they are made from nonfat milk, but most cheese products are made from whole milk high in butterfat and should be avoided. This includes cheese dips and cheese spreads of all kinds. These are usually heavy in salt and cause you to drink too much water. The salt is retained in the body cells, giving you the appearance of being bloated or fat. Many people, when dieting, believe they can eat all the cottage cheese they want, forgetting that unless it is the low-butterfat type, it is not the ideal food for losing weight.

ALL TYPES OF CALORIE–NEUTRALIZER VEGETABLES MAY BE EATEN

While you are on your lifetime, sustaining diet, you may safely eat all types of calorie–neutralizer vegetables found in priority lists no. 1 and 2. You can safely include some peas, corn, carrots and even white potatoes, if you also have a calorie-neutralizer raw vegetable salad that helps avoid absorption of the high calories. The high fiber, calorie–neutralizer vegetables that are not absorbed as fat-calories include such tasty vegetables as asparagus, artichokes, string beans, broccoli, cauliflower, mushrooms, peppers, spinach, squash, tomatoes, turnips, Brussels sprouts, eggplant and cabbage. From this long list you can prepare many tasty vegetable dishes that will help neutralize the fat calories that might be contained in your protein dishes and desserts.

Eat as many vegetables as possible raw in salads, with a low-calorie dressing, and you will receive better nutrition than if cooked. Avoid overcooking vegetables by boiling them. Instead, steam your vegetables or cook in a pressure cooker for a few minutes. This preserves their flavor and nutritive value. Serve hot with a little margarine, but avoid using heavy, rich sauces for these are usually made with cream, butter and white flour heavy in fat calories.

CALORIE–NEUTRALIZER FRUITS ARE NATURE'S FINEST DESSERTS

Most people trying to lose weight complain about having to give up sweets and rich desserts like pies, cakes, ice cream and puddings. It is true that you should not indulge your sweet tooth at the expense of your good health, even on a sustaining diet, but you can supply your body with the necessary blood sugar it needs by including fresh fruits in your daily menus as desserts.

You need never worry about cholesterol in fruits for there is none. However, if you overeat even fruit you will find yourself putting on the unwanted pounds again, for all fruits are full of natural sugars that put on weight when eaten in excess. The only fruits that do not add extra weight are cantaloupe, watermelon, strawberries, pumpkin and rhubarb. These fruits take more calories to digest than they give to the body so you can eat your fill of these without worrying about gaining weight.

Figs, dates and prunes are also a good substitute for candies, pastries and pies. Although they are high in sugar content you can safely eat three or four between meals without fear. Apples are also a good source of natural sugar and should be eaten at least once a day. If you include applesauce in your meals obtain the type that is made without sugar. Avoid honey and syrup, for they are rich in carbohydrates and are converted into fat quickly.

Eat oranges and pineapples whole, rather than drink their juices, for in digesting the pulp of the fruit you can use up most of the calories that the fruit contains. Juices of any kind, vegetable or fruit, should be avoided. They are absorbed too quickly by the body. The pulp of fruit or vegetables takes longer to digest, giving the body nutrients without adding fat calories.

USE FRUIT DESSERTS INSTEAD OF CALORIE-RICH SUGAR DESSERTS

The calorie–neutralizer diet includes such a wide variety of rich fruit desserts that you need never feel deprived of sweets. However, in the lifetime, sustaining diet, you can include some carbohydrate desserts occasionally, such as cake or ice cream, as long as it does not become a daily habit and a necessity.

THELMA W. BALLOONED TO AN INCREDIBLE 220 POUNDS IN TWO YEARS

Thelma W. was 35 years old when she began to balloon out of shape. She was the mother of two children, 5 and 8 years old. Her husband had deserted her two years before, so she was forced to work to support her children. She left them with her widowed mother while she worked. Her mother prepared all the meals and her big specialty was pies and cakes. She was considered quite an expert on desserts, as she had once won a $5,000 prize for the best cake in a national contest. The fact that her mother weighed well over 200 pounds for years did not seem to trouble Thelma, until she saw the same thing happening to her on the calorie-rich diet she ate. When Thelma reached 220 pounds, it began to interfere with her work in an assembly line soldering parts of radio sets. She realized she would have to take steps to lose weight, for her energy was sapped and she could hardly get through an eight-hour day without collapsing.

When she came into the diet workshop sessions, I analyzed Thelma's weight problem and attributed it to the psychic shock that had come when her husband left her and the two children. It was about then that Thelma began eating high-calorie desserts to compensate for her emotional loss. Thelma consumed hundreds of rich, fat calories each day, neglecting the nourishing, nonfattening meats and vegetables, and low-calorie fruits.

Although Thelma had to lose 85 pounds, I did not rush her into eliminating all sweets and desserts. I realized this would panic her and make her give up dieting completely. Instead, I gradually lowered the calorie-rich food intake and began to substitute the desserts that are made with fruits, given in Chapter 8. This satisfied her sweet tooth. In two weeks she was able to stick to the balance of the calorie–neutralizer diet without mental strain.

When she had lost 45 pounds in the first six weeks of the diet, I put her on the extension diet, including many fruits and vegetables from list no 2. This gave her a wider variety of foods from which to select. Her weight loss was a little less because the foods were richer in calories, but she still continued to lose weight. In four more weeks she had lost another 40 pounds, and then went on the sustaining diet.

It is never wise to suddenly give up calorie-rich foods, and the calorie–neutralizer diet makes allowances for the psychic shock that often comes when a person makes such a sudden change in dietary habits. That is why you should gradually substitute other low-calorie foods for the rich ones, until they become a habit.

AVOID MIXTURES OF FOODS FOR BETTER HEALTH

The chemical combinations of various foods must be carefully controlled if you wish to have good digestion. Starches digest primarily in the mouth and proteins in the stomach, so these foods should be eaten separately, not at the same meal. Citrus fruits should never be eaten with starches, as they require different digestive processes. The typical American diet is heavy in carbohydrates, starches, sugars and fats; it often causes digestive disturbances. Tons of anti-acid products are sold each year to alleviate this common problem of indigestion.

Digestive disturbances can easily be avoided by not mixing starches with acids, such as lemons, oranges, pineapple and apples, and avoiding mixing proteins, like meat, milk, cheese and eggs, with starches. Each should be eaten at different times and not mixed together at the same meal. A good example of such a mixture is eating spaghetti with tomato and meat sauce. This is why so many people cannot eat this mixture, or pizzas and lasagna without having trouble digesting them. Such mixtures often please the taste buds but wreak havoc with the digestive system. Also, it is wise to refrain from eating ice creams or sugar desserts on top of a heavy protein meat meal, for the sugars are apt to ferment before the food is digested, producing discomfort and heartburn.

INDIGESTION AND EXCESS WEIGHT
DROVE HER TO SEEK HELP

Florence J. came into the diet workshop for two reasons: One, she weighed 65 pounds more than her normal 135 pounds, and two, she suffered chronic indigestion which nothing seemed to help. Doctors had advised her to go on a diet to lose weight, as it was affecting her health and causing her to feel sluggish and constantly exhausted. As personnel director in a big firm, she had to deal with many people. She felt ungainly and awkward with all the excess weight.

First I had Florence fill out a form, giving us information on her diet. It was a surprising document. She listed daily menus consisting of mainly carbohydrate and starchy dishes, like potatoes, macaroni, white bread, plenty of butter, and rich desserts ranging from seven-layer cakes to her favorite, vanilla ice cream covered with chocolate fudge. But the starches and carbohydrates were not the worst things about her diet. She also ate plenty of fried meats, fish, chicken and lamb chops, with rich sauces and gravies.

This combination of heavy starches and proteins, with the sugar desserts on top of them, was the main cause of her attacks of indigestion. I explained to Florence that starches, sugars and carbohydrates require a different digestion from proteins such as meats, milk, cheese and fish. Mixing them together with sweet desserts brought about the attacks of indigestion she experienced. Also, this mixture tended to unbalance her metabolism, so it could no longer handle the fat content of her foods and turned it into body fat.

When Florence went on the calorie–neutralizer diet she found that her taste buds were satisfied each day. Her intake of carbohydrates and starches was so reduced that she had no digestive disturbances. This corrected the metabolic imbalance so her body could handle the calorie–neutralizer fruits, vegetables and meats without any effort.

I did not rush Florence into losing her excess weight too quickly, for that would have had repercussions in her life and work. We were satisfied to see the fat melt away at the rate of 8 to 10 pounds a week. After eight weeks she had lost the excess 65 pounds and was back to her normal weight of 135 pounds. This made such a difference in her appearance, that it encouraged Florence to go on the lifetime sustaining diet, where she could eat all the good, nourishing calorie–neutralizer foods she wanted without putting on additional weight.

AN OCCASIONAL BINGE NOT HARMFUL WHEN ON SUSTAINING DIET

When you have lost all the weight you wish and are once again back to normal, you may occasionally binge when you go to a party or restaurant where rich foods are served. If you do this once in a while you can quickly reinstate your calorie–neutralizer diet for a day or two and undo the harm that might have been done. It is only if you persist on these binges that you will soon revert to your old carbohydrate habits and gain weight again at an alarming rate. Then you have to go through the whole painful process of dieting all over again.

Make up your mind now that you will never again become addicted to the harmful, fattening carbohydrate habit that first made you gain weight. Avoid eating white bread, white sugar, white salt (use a salt substitute or a product made from sea kelp, obtained at most health food stores). Avoid overeating pies, cakes, cookies, ice cream, pizzas, lasagna, spaghetti and puddings. Eat plenty of calorie–neutalizer fruits and vegetables, meats, chicken and fish, with salads before meals to dull the appetite. You will never again fear that you will put on weight.

As an extra dividend to your normal, sustaining diet, you will see amazing benefits in your health and energy as you return to your normal weight. Not only will you feel better and enjoy life more, but you will also look more youthful when you are slender. You may live from ten to twenty years longer because you are on a sensible, balanced diet for the rest of your life.

CHAPTER 13

Questions Most Frequently Asked About the Calorie–Neutralizer Reducing Diet

Over a period of many years, I held a diet workshop in Carnegie Hall, where I lectured to 3000 people every Sunday afternoon. Literally hundreds of questions were asked concerning the calorie–neutralizer diet and problems connected with dieting in general.

When you begin any new reducing diet there are many questions you would like to ask concerning the methods used and the pros and cons of a particular dieting system. Some of the most frequently asked questions are given below. The answers will give you vital information that will prove helpful in following the calorie–neutralizer diet to lose weight.

Question 1: I once tried diet pills to lose weight but I found that they left me constantly fatigued, as I was not hungry enough to want to eat even small meals. In what ways is the calorie–neutralizer diet different from other diet methods?

Answer: It is true that diet pills contain drugs that are appetite depressants. Sometimes this method works, other times it doesn't. The reason why you were constantly tired is because you probably did not eat enough energy-producing foods to give your body the necessary nutrients to keep you going. The calorie–neutralizer diet is different because you can eat all the nonfattening food you want, and still have all the energy you need to carry out your regular life schedule. The foods in the calorie–neutralizer diet are low-calorie. You take in fewer calories than your body needs for each day and these neutralize the more fattening foods you eat.

Question 2: Should I eat between meals while on the calorie–neutralizer diet?

Answer: Yes. You can eat as many as six or even eight times a day and still continue to lose weight. You could eat up to 4 pounds of these vegetables and fruits a day and still continue to lose weight. Between-meal snacks are given that help keep your appetite under control without adding fat calories.

Question 3: Some reducing diets say to eat all the meat proteins I want. Can I do this with the calorie–neutralizer diet and continue to lose weight?

Answer: Although you can eat meat at least once or twice a day on the calorie–neutralizer diet, you can never eat all the meat you want. Even though meat is protein, it will soon add up in calories. Excess calories mean excess fat, no matter what protein foods are eaten. The only reason you can eat all of the calorie–neutralizer foods other than meat that you want is that they tend to keep the body from absorbing the fat calories. The digestive tract discards them before they can turn into fat cells. Their high-fiber, low-calorie content assures the body of sufficient nourishment without adding to the body's fat cells.

Question 4: What are calories and do I count calories on the calorie–neutralizer diet?

Answer: A calorie is the unit of heat or energy produced by any food substance. A person's age, height, weight and the type of work done are all used as indicators of the number of calories a person needs for each day's activities. For women the required calories for sedentary work ranges from 2000 to 2500. For men in sedentary work it is a little higher, from 3000 to 3500 calories. A laborer or any person who does manual work may require as many as 4000 or more calories a day, depending on the energy expended. For purposes of reducing, most diet systems call for 900 to 1200 calories per day. In the new calorie–neutralizer diet you can disregard calories. The foods given in the reducing menus are so low in fat calories you never go over the amount required for any day's activity. In fact, many people have eaten as high as 2500 calories a day and still lost weight because they ate low-fat foods in the calorie–neutralizer category. If you wish to count calories even while on the calorie–neutralizer diet, don't take in more than 1200 to 1500 calories a day. This will allow you to lose 10 to 25 pounds quickly and safely.

Question 5: Do you advocate eating grains and cereals while trying to lose weight?

Answer: Certain grains, when they are in their whole state, are included in the lists of calorie–neutralizer foods. Whole-wheat bread, protein bread, brown rice, barley, oats and soy-beans are all permitted in small quantities while on the diet. Bran is a high-fiber, calorie–neutralizer that can be used in its natural form without addition of sugar. It is valuable for the various vitamins and minerals it contains, as well as for furnishing the body with roughage that helps remove acid ash and prevent calorie absorption.

Question 6: Why is it that the diet my friend used to lose 25 pounds did not work for me? Will the calorie–neutralizer diet work for any person regardless of metabolism?

Answer: Various people have different metabolic processes than others. What worked as a diet for your friend may not work for you because your system may be so geared to carbohydrates and fats that your metabolism cannot adjust to a stringent diet in which most carbohydrates and fats are removed.

The calorie–neutralizer diet works equally well for every-one, regardless of metabolism, because some carbohydrates and fats are included in the daily menus, along with proteins, fruits, vegetables and grains. The body is never required to burn up foods and discard them faster than is normal. By slowing down the metabolism and the process of absorption, the calorie-neutralizer diet furnishes the body with sufficient energy and nutrients so you never feel starved and are never low in blood sugar and energy. If all carbohydrates are removed from a diet you would soon become fatigued and feel constantly famished.

Question 7: My mother, father, two sisters, brother and I are all heavy. Isn't it natural for some families to be heavy, and isn't it an inherited trait to be fat? My mother told me that it was a glandular condition that we can do nothing about. Shouldn't we accept our burden of fat as being natural and not work so hard to diet and reduce?

Answer: There are several false assumptions implied in this question and its elaborate evasiveness. First of all, a person's various bodily faults and limitations are not necessarily hereditary, just as most diseases are not hereditary. However, a tendency to be fat does run in many families—not because of a glandular condition, but because the families' habit patterns over several generations run to eating heavily of carbohydrates, sugars and starches and foods high in fat content. These eating habits that are in some families do affect the glands, for the metabolism is changed and begins to set up a craving for the fatty foods that will feed the fat deposits that have accumulated in the body. Fat cells do not like to die. They scream for sugars, starches, fats and carbohydrates to keep them alive, neglecting the low-fat foods that include vegetables, fruits and many meats.

The calorie–neutralizer diet recognizes the body's legitimate needs for proteins, fats and carbohydrates. The reducing menus apportion each day's food to include small amounts of fats and carbohydrates, with the various calorie–neutralizer vegetables, fruits and grains that hold back the fat absorption to a minimum. Soon the digestive tract and the metabolism become accustomed to this normal pattern of eating nourishing, nonfattening foods and adjust to the new healthy method of eating.

Question 8: I have heard that white sugar, white flour and white salt are all fattening and harmful. Is this true and does the new calorie–neutralizer diet give us substitutes for these?

Answer: Yes, it is true that white flour and refined or white sugar are high in calories. When overeaten they tend to add many fat calories to the body. As to white salt, I advocate using a salt substitute. The usual table salt is known chemically as sodium chloride, and is a poison when too much is taken. It tends to dissolve and remain in the body's cells where water accumulates, giving the body a bloated, fat appearance. Some scientists believe that it can be harmful to the health and lead to high blood pressure, heart trouble and arthritis. There is a form of sea kelp which many use for a salt substitute, and you can also use the calorie–neutralizer vegetables such as celery, string beans, zucchini, lettuce and others, which are high in sodium content. It is sodium the body needs, not sodium chloride. Whole-wheat flour may be used instead of white flour. Sugars may be obtained from the calorie–neutralizer fruits given in the diet, and also from dried or fresh prunes, apricots, peaches, apples, dates and figs.

Question 9: Should I take supplemental vitamins and minerals while I am on the calorie–neutralizer diet?

Answer: Scientists and nutritionists agree that everyone requires certain vitamins and minerals to keep healthy and vigorous. Although I advocate that these vitamins and minerals should be taken in the natural calorie–neutralizer foods given in our menus, each person must decide what is best for him or her. If in doubt about not getting the proper amount of vitamins in your diet it is always wise to consult your physician. If you eat a wide variety of the calorie–neutralizer meats, fruits, grains and vegetables, you are certain to obtain the required amounts of vitamins that have been judged necessary to good health and nutrition.

Question 10: Although I am a vegetarian I constantly gain weight because I love to eat sweet things like ice cream, cakes, pies, cookies and soft drinks. I am also fond of pizza, spaghetti and lasagna. Is the calorie–neutralizer diet for meat eaters alone or can a vegetarian also use it?

Answer: A true vegetarian who does not have a strong carbohydrate habit, but sticks to vegetables, grains, fruits and seeds, is rarely ever fat. The fact that you admit to a strong craving for sweets and carbohydrates is proof that your weight problem is due to these fat-calorie foods. If you use the calorie–neutralizer diet to lose your extra pounds you will soon break yourself of the vicious carbohydrate habit that is ruining the health of millions of Americans. Your vegetarian diet would be perfect for maintaining your body in good health with your right weight. I suggest that vegetarians use milk and milk products to obtain more of the proteins that are essential to good health.

Question 11: I enjoy eating certain foods that I know are starchy, such as corn, potatoes and rice. Do I need to give them up to go on the calorie–neutralizer diet?

Answer: White rice, corn and potatoes are all carbo-hydrates. In the calorie–neutralizer diet I urge giving up these foods until the required weight has been lost. Brown rice happens to be more of a protein than a carbohydrate. It can be eaten with meats, fish and chicken, as well as the calorie–neutralizer vegetables, grains and fruits, while losing weight. If corn and potatoes are eaten the carbohydrate effect can be neutralized by eating at least two of the calorie–neutralizer vegetables in the same meal.

Question 12: Our family has always served wine with our meals. I admit I am very much overweight and I want to go on the calorie–neutralizer diet to lose weight. Will I have to give up wine with my meals?

Answer: If your problem is only 10 to 20 pounds, you need not worry about giving up wine with your meals, for you will only need to diet about two weeks to lose that weight. However, if you have a more severe problem then you should cut out wine, beer, cocktails, and most alcoholic drinks until you have shed the desired pounds, for most alcoholic beverages are high in calories.

Question 13: Are most fruits fattening?

Answer: All foods, including fruits, are fattening if eaten in large quantities. However, in the calorie–neutralizer diet there are several fruits which can be eaten in large quantities without adding fat: cantaloupe, watermelon, strawberries, apples, rhubarb and pumpkin. You can eat your fill of these, as they require more calories to digest than they give to the body. Limit the quantity you eat of other fruits. Oranges should be eaten whole, for the pulp resists the digestive process and keeps the body from absorbing the calories. Grapefruit should also be eaten pulp and juice together. Most fruits are high in sugar, so they do tend to increase weight if eaten in large quantities. Limit them in the calorie–neutralizer diet until the required weight has been lost. On the lifetime sustaining diet you can include all fruits if you eat them in small quantities.

Question 14: When I was a child my mother gave me lots of candy and soda pop. Now I am a mother and have three children who all demand candy and soft drinks. I remember my bad teeth and know it was due to sweets. How can I satisfy my children's craving for sweets without endangering their health or making them fatties?

Answer: The calorie–neutralizer diet satisfies the sweet tooth by serving plenty of fresh or canned fruits for desserts. You might try giving your children raisins mixed with nuts, or figs, dates, candy made with honey and fruits, and prunes, apricots and peaches that have been dried and soaked in water. You can also satisfy their sweet tooth by giving your children low-calorie puddings and special desserts that come in powered form.

Question 15: Can I eat all the eggs I want on the calorie–neutralizer diet? Is the cholesterol from eggs as bad as many claim?

Answer: I suggest that eggs be eaten only two or three times a week while dieting, not only because of their cholesterol level, but because they are so quickly digested and absorbed in the digestive tract. However, when eggs are given in the reducing menus I suggest two calorie–neutralizer fruits or vegetables be eaten in the same meal. Eggs should be poached or boiled, seldom fried.

Question 16: My husband is 55 pounds overweight. He likes fat on meat and eats all of his as well as mine. Is this making him fat?

Answer: The fat in meat is high in calories; it should be cut off before the meat is cooked. Although fat in itself does not necessarily make you fat, eating too much of it will certainly add so many fat calories that you will inevitably put on weight. In the calorie–neutralizer diet all fat is trimmed from the meat. I suggest that fat intake be cut down to a little salad oil, about a tablespoonful a day. Some oil or fat is necessary for proper metabolism, but it can be overdone, as in your husband's case, and this leads to becoming overweight. In the normal, sustaining diet for maintaining the correct weight we suggest some fats taken in moderation as being necessary to perfect metabolism. The fats from heavy cream are not as bad as you might think. Whole milk actually is more fattening.

Question 17: My husband of 15 years is not very potent. He weighs 195 pounds and is now 25 pounds overweight. Could this be affecting his sexual potency?

Answer: Scientists have found that the sexual drive in both men and women seems to lessen when a person is excessively fat. This could be true in your husband's case, although I suspect it may have something to do with his actual food intake. If he neglects eating the foods that stimulate sexual activity, he may be missing out on vitamins and minerals that are considered essential to the proper functioning of the reproductive tract. This includes lecithin, which can be obtained by using soybean oil, soybean flour and soybean powder in baking breads and cakes. You may also obtain lecithin by eating sunflower, sesame and pumpkin seeds. The most important mineral for increasing sexual potency is manganese, which can be obtained in calorie–neutralizer foods such as whole grains, cereals and green vegetables.

Question 18: I have had a weight problem for the past ten years. I try various diets and am able to lose from 10 to 20 pounds in a short time, but the moment I stop the diet I regain the weight. Will the calorie–neutralizer reducing diet assure me I will never again put on weight?

Answer: No guarantee can be given that the calorie–neutralizer reducing diet will keep you from ever putting weight on again. The normal sustaining diet given in Chapter 12 gives you a method by which you can eat the right foods to maintain your normal weight. However, if you return to your old habits of eating mainly carbohydrate foods above the 60 grams required amount, you will quickly put on the pounds you have lost. If you adopt the calorie–neutralizer sustaining diet as a way of life, you need never again fear putting on excess weight. If you find that at times you have splurged and eaten too many forbidden carbohydrates, you can reinstate the calorie–neutralizer reducing diet for a few days and lose the extra pounds. The sustaining calorie–neutralizer diet gives you such a wide variety of foods to choose from that you need never worry about being deprived or going hungry to maintain your normal weight for life.

Question 19: I am 25 years old, female, 5 feet 6 inches tall, and weigh what is supposed to be normal for my age and height. How many calories should I eat each day to maintain normal weight? I am an office worker.

Answer: Your age, height and type of work require about 2600 calories a day to maintain normal weight. However, if these calories are carbohydrate in nature, or fat calories instead of lean calories, you will probably gain weight in the future. Cut out the fat calories and you will find that you can then eat up to 3000 calories a day without putting on extra weight. If your food intake is made up of starches, sugars, fats and high-calorie meats, you will find yourself gaining weight. This will be especially true after the age of 30. To safeguard against this happening, begin now to choose your foods from the low-calorie lists given in this diet system.

Question 20: If I go on the calorie–neutralizer diet to lose my extra pounds, how can I kill my hunger pangs? Most diets I have tried give such small amounts of food that I feel constantly starved.

Answer: There are many low-calorie foods in the calorie–neutralizer diet that you can eat as between-meal snacks. You can eat as many as six or even eight times a day, if you stick with the low-calorie foods, and never suffer from hunger pangs. Keep a plate of celery stalks, radishes, sliced tomatoes, cucumbers and lettuce in the refrigerator and munch on these when hungry. You can also keep leftover meats, fish and poultry to use as between-meal snacks. Also, you can have a bowl of delicious soup made from calorie–neutralizer vegetables such as tomatoes, cabbage, green peppers, onions and celery, sprinkled on top with Parmesan cheese. This is a good appetite suppressor and adds few calories to the body. You could also eat your fill of cantaloupe, honeydew melon and watermelon, in season, and not add one ounce of weight. Strawberries, apples, rhubarb (cooked with artificial sugar) and pumpkin are all fruits that kill appetites and add no calories. All you need to remember is not to eat calorie–rich foods like ice cream, pies, cakes, cookies, pizza, spaghetti, lasagna or fruits that are in our high-calorie lists. These would increase the sugar in your body and be stored as extra weight.

Index